M. Gidley

The Vanishing Race

Selections from Edward S. Curtis'
The North American Indian

University of Washington Press

Seattle

Douglas & McIntyre

Vancouver/Toronto

In memory of my father
GUSTAVUS GIDLEY, 1900–1974

Introduction copyright © 1976 by M. Gidley
Preface to the Paperback Edition copyright © 1987 by M. Gidley
Printed in the United State of America

First paperback edition published in 1987 by the University of Washington
Press, Seattle, and by Douglas & McIntyre, 1615 Venables Street, Vancouver,
British Columbia V5L 2H1

Library of Congress Cataloging-in-Publication Data

Curtis, Edward S., 1868-1952.
  The vanishing race.

  Reprint. Originally published: Newton Abbot,
England: David & Charles, c1976.
  Bibliography: p.
  Includes index.
  1. Indians of North America. I. Gidley, M.
(Mick) II. Title.
[E77.C982   1987]   973′.0497   87-14263
ISBN 0-295-96513-4 (pbk.)

Canadian Cataloguing in Publication Data

Curtis, Edward S., 1868-1952.
  The vanishing race

  Originally published: Newton Abbot [England]:
David & Charles, 1976.
  Includes index.
  ISBN 0-88894-582-5
  1. Indians of North America. I. Gidley, M.
(Mick). II. Curtis, Edward S., 1868-1952.
The North American Indian. III. Title.
E77.C87 1987   970.004′97   C87-091107-4

Title page photo: Cañon de Chelly, a Navajo stronghold

Contents

List of Illustrations

Preface
to the Paperback Edition

The work for the original edition of this book, the first and the fullest comprehensive selection from Edward S. Curtis' *The North American Indian,* was completed more than ten years ago. Fortunately, I think that I would still reach substantially the same decisions about the selection itself—though I would also continue to argue for a larger sum total of pages in order to include more long items. If the letters I have received from some of the book's readers are anything to go by, it has served its primary purpose in making a major work of scholarship accessible to many people who would not have the time or the inclination to spend days or, even, weeks in a major research library absorbing the complete twenty-volume opus.

Since 1976, when *The Vanishing Race* was first published, a number of other works on Curtis have appeared, including *Edward S. Curtis in the Land of the War Canoes* (1980) by Bill Holm and George I Quimby. If the economics of the present operation had allowed, I would definitely have augmented this book's brief Bibliographical Notes. Also, I have continued to research *The North American Indian* project for essays and a longer study of my own, so that—if it is not too immodest to say so—I now know considerably more about it than I did then. This means that while I am only irritatingly aware of certain minor errors in the Map and the Index, there are some emphases in the Introduction itself that I would have wished to put right: the whole Curtis enterprise was more collaborative and the notion of Indians as "a vanishing race" had greater complexity than appears there. Also, the terms of expressions used in the final paragraph, though I continue to support their stress, sound somewhat chauvinistic to my current state of consciousness.

I would like to take this opportunity to repeat my thanks to those who assisted me in the production of the original edition: Roy Batten, Joy Brown, June Cooling, Heather Eva, Florence Curtis Graybill, Phoebe Harris, W. Hoskin, Allen Koppenhaver, John Stirling, Carol Thomas, June Thomas, and Mike Weaver. I also wish to thank Exeter University Library again for allowing the use of its set of *The North American Indian,* John Saunders for his photographic work, and Naomi Pascal of the University of Washington Press for her encouragement. My debts to Nancy, my wife, continue to be beyond annotation here.

The original edition of this book was dedicated to the memory of my father, Gustavus Gidley (1900-1974), and I would like to renew that inadequate gesture.

MICK GIDLEY
Exeter, January 1987

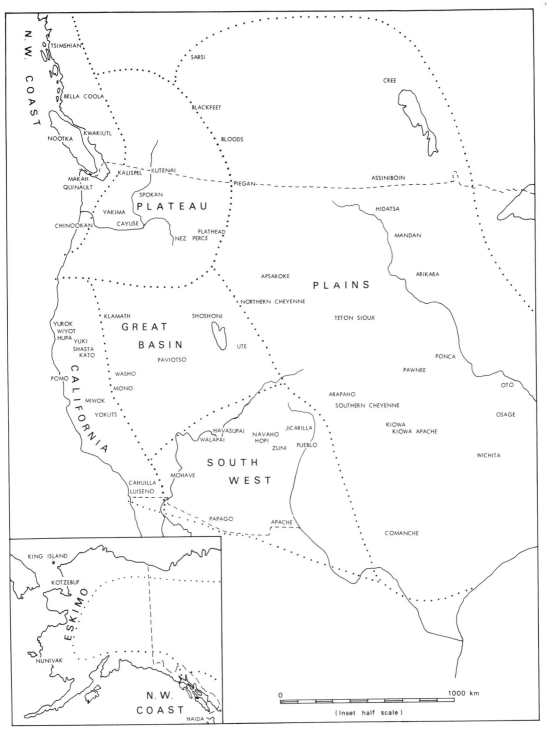

North American Indians as
witnessed by Edward S. Curtis:
tribal locations and culture areas
in the United States (including,
inset, Alaska) and Canada

Introduction

Edward S. Curtis (1868-1952) and
The North American Indian

When the Spanish conquistadors appeared on their
horizons in the sixteenth century, elders of the Hopi
Indians advanced to greet the soldiers in the belief that the
Spaniards were representatives of their long lost white
brother. Contacts between whites and Indians like this—
together with encounters which proved bloody from the
start, such as with the Comanche—brought the North
American Indian into the consciousness of Europeans, and
into the consciousness of those Europeans who, through the
formative experiences associated with migration across seas
and settlement in strange lands, became Americans. The
whites at once started to mythologise: the Indians who
helped the Mayflower settlers survive their first winter in
the New World became noble savages, those who
threatened Captain John Smith with execution became
bloodthirsty villains and those who exchanged Manhattan
Island for a few beads and trinkets became both fools and
benefactors.

Thus many different peoples speaking hundreds of
distinct languages and living in environments ranging from
sunken deserts to tropical swamp, from wooded mountains
to bone bare plains, were remade into one complex but
composite image of the Redskin, *the* Indian. And during
the period of most rapid expansion westwards in the
nineteenth century, though particular tribes were singled
out for public acknowledgement in that their names—
Sioux, Cheyenne, Apache, Nez Percé—became bywords for
savage fighting (or, at best, resistance), the individual
qualities of the cultures of these and other distinctly
different peoples became further fused, subsumed into the
one overwhelming myth of *the* Indian, invariably a
painted plainsman about to swoop with bloodcurdling
yells onto an unsuspecting waggon train of sturdy yeomen
wanting only to start a new life. Moreover, as all of us

1 *Princess Angeline*, daughter
of Chief Seattle. She was a
familiar figure on the streets
of the city in Curtis' early
manhood

9

who have watched films and television can testify, such imagery has dominated the white consciousness until very recently.

But when the seeming white brother appeared on the mesas of Arizona in the sixteenth century, the Hopi had been expecting him for hundreds of years. Indeed, nearly all of the Indian peoples—however much the coming of horses and other later imports affected the bases of their cultures—had a history, a religion, a system of government, social customs, handicrafts, and myths and songs of their own which predated the coming of white people amongst them. Edward Sheriff Curtis' *The North American Indian*, from which all the materials in this book have been selected, was a truly magnificent effort to record a vast amount of very many of these aboriginal cultures. Published between 1907 and 1930 in twenty volumes of illustrated text and twenty portfolios containing more than seven hundred large-sized photogravures, *The North American Indian*, which was issued in an edition of only five hundred ar.d sold rather expensively on a subscription basis, contains millions of words: descriptions of homelands; accounts of religious beliefs that some of us might find strange; accounts of tribal organisations ranging from the aristocratic to the casually democratic; records of ceremonies so subtle in their significance, or so bizarre, that an alien eyewitness could easily not understand what it all meant; versions of haunting myths, songs and stories; descriptions of intricate and skilled arts and hunting practices; and heroic tales of arms and men. In short. *The North American Indian* is a monument in words and pictures to a range of cultures which most white men could not or would not see.

It is also a monument to the zeal and stamina of its producer, Edward S. Curtis. Curtis was born near Whitewater, Wisconsin, but grew to manhood in the environs of Seattle, Washington; his father, Johnson, had joined the great westward migration in search of a better life. In 1855, when Chief Seattle surrendered the Puget Sound region on which the city was to be built, he said in his address to Governor Isaac Stevens, 'When the last Red Men shall have perished, and the memory of my tribe shall have become a myth among the white man, these shores will swarm with the invisible dead of my tribe, and when your children's children think themselves

2 Edward S. Curtis, self portrait, c1910

10

alone in the field, the store, the shop, or in the silence of
the pathless woods, they will not be alone.' During
Curtis' youth Seattle was a frontier town, confident,
heaving and building, yet still in fact frequented by some
few dispossessed Indians, including Princess Angeline,
Chief Seattle's daughter. Seattle was also a port, and the
combination of frontier city and the opening to the sea
presented the energetic young Curtis, who had already
taught himself photography, with opportunities for both
advancement and travel. He was quick, for example, to
follow and report on the hardships which befell the
prospectors who joined the gold rush to the Klondike in
1897.

There was much business—and much which held interest
—for a Pacific Northwest photographer at the turn of the
century, as is evidenced by the documentation of logging
by Darius Kinsey and the recording of scenery by Curtis'
brother, Asahel. By 1892 Edward Curtis was a partner in
a studio, and *his* favourite subjects were Mount Rainier,
city scenes, and local Indians. He considered these
aboriginal people as decadent and lost, but his pictures of
them began to win prizes in competitions. One weekend
while climbing and photographing, he rescued a party of
travellers stranded on Mount Rainier. Among them was
George Bird Grinnell, an authority on Indians. Through
Grinnell, who befriended him, Curtis was appointed
Official Photographer to the Harriman Alaska Expedition
of 1899. During this survey, though Curtis was
impressed by the leader, C. Hart Merriam, and by John
Muir, an originator of the National Park idea (and author
of, for example, *The Mountains of California*, which Curtis
was later to quote), the influence on him of Grinnell
deepened and he agreed to accompany the older man on
his annual visit to the Piegan Sun Dance ceremonies the
following year.

In the course of these rituals of pain willingly suffered
'for strength and visions', Curtis appears to have experienced
a sense of mystical communion with the Indians, and out
of it came his conception of a comprehensive written and
photographic record of the most important Indian peoples
west of the Mississippi and Missouri Rivers who still
retained 'to a considerable degree their primitive customs
and traditions.' Curtis seems to have held to a varying
but always paradoxical racial ideology. On the one hand,

like most white men of his day, he believed that when measured against the doctrine of 'the survival of the fittest' the Indians were revealed as unadaptable, even inferior, and thus he could cast down judgements as if from superiority, as he does, for instance, when he says 'no single noble trait redeems the Kwakiutl character.' On the other hand, out of his understanding of individuals and cultures, he regretted and elegised the Indians' passing, chose 'The Vanishing Race'—his view of some Navahos entering a canyon, one head turned to look regretfully back—as the keynote picture for the whole of *The North American Indian*, and grew to respond to his government's policy towards Indians—which he saw not as inevitable but chosen—with fierce anger (as may be witnessed here in the section on U.S. Government treatment of the Indians of California).

In the light of the emergence of the American Indian Movement and other present day manifestations of 'Red Consciousness', perhaps Curtis was too pessimistic in

3 *The Vanishing Race.* Curtis thought this picture captured the emotion which inspired his whole enterprise in *The North American Indian*

feeling that the Indians had no definable future as Indians; however, he was certainly correct in his judgement that he was living at a time which was the last possible one for many memories to be recorded (such as those here of the Apsaroke, Hunts to Die) and for many images to be captured by his magic box (such as the faces of figures like Little Wolf and Red Cloud or the celebration of ceremonies like that of placating the spirit of a slain eagle). Although married with a growing family, Curtis embarked on a task that lasted thirty years, that took him in heat and snow to the remoter regions of a continent, and to which he frequently devoted over seventeen hours a day. With a team of regular assistants that included W. E. Myers as his right hand man, and which was often augmented by valuable Indian informants like A. B. Upshaw and Jackson, his interpreter among the Eskimos, Curtis set out to produce his major work, *The North American Indian*.

Despite popular exhibitions, lantern slide lectures, and

4 Curtis' camp among the Walapai, near the Grand Cañon in Arizona

13

5 A. B. Upshaw, an educated
Apsaroke, was invaluable to
Curtis as an interpreter
among several Plains peoples

contracts for magazine articles, by 1905 Curtis had run out
of funds. But his photographs had attracted attention.
President Theodore Roosevelt employed him to
take his daughter's wedding pictures and then financier
J. Pierpont Morgan, out of his virtually uncountable
fortune, agreed to subsidise the field work and book
production costs for *The North American Indian* by granting
the capital to set up a company, The North American
Indian Inc. Frederick Webb Hodge, perhaps *the* leading
authority on Indians then, agreed to edit the volumes, and
Roosevelt himself wrote a Foreword in which he praised
Curtis' powers of observation, both of external facts and of

'that strange spiritual and mental life' of his subjects.
Curtis returned to the field with renewed vigour,
sometimes accompanied by such notables as Edmond S.
Meany, historian of Washington State, or A. C. Haddon,
virtual founder in Britain of anthropology as an
academic discipline. He caught thousands of images, wrote
score upon score of words, and even made a film—
In the Land of the Headhunters (1914)—which in some
respects anticipates Robert Flaherty's conception of
narrative documentary in *Nanook of the North* (1920).

Curtis wanted *The North American Indian*—with its oral
histories, detailed tribal summaries, occasional hand-
coloured pictures, language data, transcriptions of music
(which had been recorded on phonographic cylinders),
native designs, and other constituents which cannot be
adequately represented in the present book—to be both
the most comprehensive compendium possible and to
present, in essence, nothing less than the very spirit of the
Indian peoples. He accordingly consumed quantities of
energy and patience on his subjects, spending weeks at a
time with them, returning year after year to acquire the
information and pictures he needed, persuading them to
re-enact ceremonies and events and to let him witness
sacred occasions. Yet he also somehow found time to tout
for subscriptions on the Eastern seaboard and to take stills
for Cecil B. de Mille's *The Ten Commandments* (1923).
The final volume, on the Eskimos of Alaska, was published
in 1930. After this, his health broken by the incessant
travel and strain, Curtis moved his studio to Los Angeles,
and in his later years watched his life's work seemingly
slide into oblivion, became interested in mining and
dreamed of an expedition to the interior gold mines of
South America.

The North American Indian—expensively produced (with
many of its photogravures printed on tissue paper), issued
in a severely limited edition over a long period—*could* not
prove popular. But in recent years anthropologists and
others, even when they have censured Curtis'
methodological assumptions or quarrelled with his
conclusions, have begun to appreciate the value of his
achievement; exhibitions have been mounted, anthologies
of pictures have been published, and his writings have been
increasingly cited in other men's researches. There has
already been a reprint edition of Curtis' entire work and

there will doubtless be scholarly editions of parts of *The
North American Indian* complete with annotation
incorporating the findings of more recent authorities,
but the present book aims to perform a different function.
Intended primarily for the general reader, it is the first
publication of a selection from *The North American Indian*
of both words and pictures; it offers in short compass—
shorter than any one of the original twenty volumes—
the range and quality of what Curtis himself called his
'national undertaking'. Curtis was a vigorous and precise
writer, and I have therefore tried to keep editorial
interference to a minimum. However, some selections
have been silently abbreviated by block cutting of
paragraphs and, sometimes, of ends or beginnings of
paragraphs (though all cuts within the paragraph, usually
of Indian words or references to other parts of *The North
American Indian* that the reader hasn't seen, are
indicated by ellipses); in a very few instances I have
summarised passages of detail in a couple of sentences and
these, like other editorial additions, whether using words
or information provided by Curtis elsewhere or not,
appear in square brackets; also, many inessential words in
Indian languages have been removed, as many of the
ellipses signify (though it should not be thought that the
remaining transcriptions, minus the complicated and
non-reproducible orthography Curtis invented, are
anything more than a very rough guide to their
pronunciation). The motivation for these changes to
Curtis' text—with the exception of printing some song
words without their accompanying music—was solely my
belief that a reader would be better served by a selection
of very many characteristic short extracts than by fewer
longer ones.

Thus, there is something here from each of the original
twenty volumes; the numbers in roman and arabic
numerals at the end of each selection indicate,
respectively, the volume and page(s) of *The North
American Indian* from which the extract has been taken
and the date of publication is given in parentheses. Very
many peoples are represented, but even so several
important groups are slighted, including the Mandan,
Nez Percé, Yakima, Arapaho, and Papago tribes. Also,
because of an attempt to cover as many peoples as
possible under each of the chosen headings, longer and

more cumulative discussions could not be excerpted, and thus examples of the exceedingly rich ceremonial life of, say, the Hopi people, had to be sacrificed, as did accounts of Sun Dance rituals, of the white man's slaughter of the buffalo, and a more varied sample of forms of tribal organisation. Curtis stated that the objective of *The North American Indian* was to depict 'all features of Indian life and environment . . . the young and the old, with their habitations, industries, ceremonies, games, and everyday customs,' and to this list could be added such matters as the history, religion, mythology, and stories of each people. Thus many kinds of writing are to be found in Curtis' work—anthropology and biography, polemic and history, folklore, and so on. The present book aims to include these kinds, and, moreover, is organised to closely reflect Curtis' own fundamental arrangement for each of his volumes. This means that some peoples are not met with until later in this organisation; therefore, as the reader will not necessarily have any primary facts about them, such as their homeland or linguistic grouping, a map of where Curtis located each people is included and the Index gives basic data for each tribe mentioned. There are also brief Bibliographical Notes.

Of his own photographs Curtis said, 'rather than being designed for mere embellishment,' they are 'each an illustration of an Indian character or of some vital phase in his existence.' Sometimes the relationship of picture to text is direct, as in the portrait of Two Strike, whose Biographical Sketch in Volume III reads as follows:

> Brulé. Born 1821. At the age of twelve he accompanied his first war-party against Pawnee. At thirty-one he led a party against the same tribe and counted coup. Twelve coups, all on Pawnee, and twenty-two battles. Two Pawnee counted coup on him, but the second he killed. Was never wounded. Name changed from Living Bear to Two Strike after unhorsing two Pawnee riding the same animal. After the sixth coup he was declared chief, and, as others died, gradually ascended to the position of head-chief of the Brulés. He never fasted for the purpose of seeing a vision, and had no medicine, but wore a bear's ear 'to frighten the enemy'.

In the present book the pictures sometimes act as direct illustration in this way, and sometimes as variations on the themes of the chapters in which they appear, but never as 'mere embellishment'. The very composition of a picture like 'The Cañon de Chelly' has much to tell: without reducing the Cañon's scale or harsh grandeur, the photograph stresses the fact that it is *home* to the Indians who transverse its floor. Or, again, in 'The Fire Drill' the movement of lines and the play of textures in the foot of the tree, in the man's apparel, in the twigs in his hair, in the very lines of his face, all betoken that he is as rooted in that land as the tree by which he squats.

The documentary and aesthetic impulses are inextricably expressed to perfection in Curtis' works—especially the portraits. When the western person looks at Curtis' view of Kenowun, a Nunivak Eskimo, he cannot but be aware that a representative of an alien society returns his gaze—the very accoutrements of her culture dangle between, threatening to hinder a relationship. Yet she is seen close up: her essential humanity smiles through. To expand our vision of Man by presenting, via words and pictures, western Indian peoples in their wondrous varieties: this is Curtis' ultimate achievement. If the Indians are a vanishing race—and Kenowun, for one, inheritor of a harsh existence and photographed in 1928, is surely dead now—it is my conviction that they also partake of immortality in Curtis' pages; indeed, with Curtis' words and pictures in our minds we modern western men truly will never be 'alone'—if in a different sense to that predicted by Chief Seattle—and our sense of the human family is enhanced.

I General Description

The Comanche

The Comanche are the sole representatives of the Shoshonean stock in Oklahoma. Like most of the tribes in that state, they were not natives of it, but were placed there for riddance. However, they differed from most other tribes removed to Oklahoma in that they were not strangers to the region, for it had been part of their hunting and raiding grounds for many years. No North American tribe ranged over so broad a territory. The Comanche were without prejudice in their selection of victims.

Fragmentary tradition collected from the present Comanche indicates that prior to their knowledge of the white race their central habitat was about the headwaters of the Platte river in what is now Wyoming. At that period the Comanche and the Shoshone were no doubt one aggregation, and at a somewhat earlier date had been a mountain people, but with increasing numbers they grew in boldness and moved out on the plains. Jealousy among chiefs and factional strife were responsible for the tribal division which became a permanent separation.

The movement of the group which became known as the Comanche was southwardly. No doubt one factor which influenced the southerly migration was the presence of horses in that direction, introduced by the Spaniards about a hundred and fifty years earlier. By the beginning of the eighteenth century raids by the Comanche extended well into Mexico, and for nearly two centuries they were at the height of their savage glory. By natural accretion and by raiding they accumulated great herds of horses, which afforded to them a freedom of movement not hitherto enjoyed. Their vast domain was dotted with buffalo, which solved the problem of the food quest with a minimum of effort. Their hunting range and raiding territory may be likened to a broadly extended oval with its northern point on the South Platte river in northern Colorado, its southern point well down in Mexico, its western border the Rio Grande in New Mexico, and its eastern limit the hills of Arkansas. In all that region, a veritable empire, the Comanche had no friends.

It would seem that a life characterized by constant warfare would have reduced their numbers materially, but when it is considered that the principal purpose of their raids was the capture of horses and women, the maintenance of a vigorous and increasing population was not difficult. The problem of feeding a multiplicity of wives was readily solved by the plenitude of buffalo, which supplied also clothing and shelter, as well as almost every other need. Every woman was an expert in tanning. The larger a man's household, the richer he was.

In the early part of the eighteenth century a favorite object of Comanche raids was Pecos and other villages of the peaceful Pueblo Indians of New Mexico; but of these, Pecos on the eastern frontier was the chief sufferer. The principal pueblo of the Southwest in the middle of the sixteenth century, Pecos time and again was so persistently and viciously attacked that the ultimate abandonment by its few survivors in 1838 was due largely to this cause. In the last important raid on Pecos, the Comanche, according to their own admission, killed fully half of the male population and almost all the old women, and carried off more than a hundred female prisoners.

The Comanche were especially hostile toward Mexicans and Mexican Indians. They regarded the Mexicans and Indians of New Mexico as Mexican in nationality, and in recounting their warlike deeds lay great stress on their forays against the 'Karisses,' among whom the Texans are included. Thus American pioneers in Texas fell heir to this situation, and for a generation constant conflict existed between the people of Texas and the Comanche, with the result that the Indians were ultimately driven from the state. With Americans other than those of Texas, the Comanche seemingly felt that they had no quarrel, hence usually were inclined to avoid conflict. Following the tribal peace with the Kiowa, about 1795, however, they were at times drawn into hostility with the American frontiersmen.

The Kiowa were as inherently hostile to the Americans as were the Comanche toward the Texans and Mexicans. When the Kiowa first moved into the south and came in contact with the Comanche, there followed some years of bitter intertribal hostility which proved so disastrous to both that their chiefs decided it would be better to hunt and fight in alliance than to continue the decimating warfare among themselves. This peace, broken at times through minor dissension, has continued to the present day. The agreement, the Comanche say, was brought about by the effort of a trader whom they called Saparit. The head-chief of the Comanche at that time was Pathiago; of the Kiowa, Sechare.

The Comanche are a striking example of the variant characteristics which develop from a parent group. The majority of the tribes belonging to the Shoshonean stock, so far as inherent tendencies are concerned, are the antithesis of the Comanche with their fearless blood lust. Truly there is a vast difference between these vigorous, proud rovers of the plains and the lowly Paiute of the deserts of eastern California and Nevada; and an even greater difference exists between them and the mild-voiced Hopi of Arizona, yet they all spring from the same parent group.

Ethnologically the Comanche do not furnish a fertile field of inquiry. The old men, when questioned as to the dearth of ceremonies, folktales, and legends such as existed, for example, with the Wichita and neighboring tribes, made answer, 'We were hunters and warriors, and had no time to think of such matters.' All information gathered from them indicates that they were so active in warfare, so constantly on the move, that they had little time to give thought to the origin and purpose of their existence; in fact, they seemingly took pride in not doing so.

This lack of cultural development was understood by the tribes with whom the Comanche had contact. Said the wise men of neighboring tribes, 'The Comanche do not know anything; they do not think'; by which they meant that the Comanche possessed no 'spiritual knowledge,' rather than that they were ignorant of anything pertaining to warfare, the chase, and other temporal matters. It is true that the Comanche had the germ of the usual beliefs in supernatural beings—of good and evil spirits—but there is no knowledge that their religious concepts were highly developed. Sedentary tribes usually gave more thought to religious beliefs and ceremonies than did the wanderers, among which no Indians were more noted than the Comanche. Few ceremonies were held by them, yet they had the Sun dance, and, as might be expected, went to great extremes in self-torture. In this ceremony they used songs borrowed from other tribes. The customary Sun-dance lodge was not built; they employed instead a large tipi made by using broadly extended poles and overlaying them with several lodge-covers.

The Comanche had also a somewhat elaborate healing rite, known as the 'Big Tail Medicine' ceremony, which had its origin in a vision. It is said that a man was fasting in the mountains and in his dream the beaver taught him how to heal the sick. On his return to camp he initiated the healing rite as instructed in the vision, and if he made no mistake in following the divine teachings, the ailing one recovered. Any one with a sick relative could ask the 'Big Tail healer' to perform the healing rite, promising the customary gifts if the patient was cured.

For this rite a large oblong tipi was erected, the poles and covering of two ordinary tipis being combined. This lodge was prepared the day preceding the ceremony. At the east a deep trench was dug to symbolize the underground runway of the beaver. In the centre of the tipi was a pool of water, with willow branches and a small willow tree planted at its western margin. At the left on entering the lodge was an earthen mound in the form of a beaver. Directly west of this effigy mound and near the

rear wall was a beaver-shape mound of earth on which the patient rested. The giver of the ceremony was a relative of the patient, who first interviewed the healer. Preceding the opening of the rite, the healer and giver entered; next the patient was brought in and placed upon the prepared mound, and then the women filed in, taking their positions in two equal groups at the north and south sides. These were followed by the men, who took their places in a line directly behind the women. Next came the singers, who were seated in two lines in front of the women. Lastly, the healer's assistants in single file came to the entrance and halted. The leader whirled his 'thunder-maker' or bullroarer. (A bullroarer is a thin oblong piece of wood tied to one end of a string about six feet long. By whirling this rapidly, a roaring sound is produced. This implement is used in many Pueblo rites to simulate thunder. The movement of the line of men in circling the lodge is in every way suggestive of Pueblo ceremonies.)

The assistants encircled the lodge, stopping at each cardinal point until the leader whirled his thunder-maker, and then took their places in two lines in front of the singers. As soon as they were seated, the ceremonial pipe was smoked by the assistants, but not by the healer. The giver of the rite then approached the healer, offering prayers to him that he might heal the ailing one and reiterating his promise of gifts if successful. The healer, presumably following the instructions of the beaver, treated the patient by the usual routine of incantation, manipulation of the body, and removal of the evil by sucking. Following this somewhat long treatment, the singers rendered four songs. At midday all adjourned until night, when the ceremony was repeated, and it was again performed the next day and night—provided, of course, the patient survived the ordeal. Between each series of healing rites the patient was carried about the camp to various tipis, the procession being led by the assistants and the thunder-maker. Whether this public exhibition of the patient was associated with the thought of producing a beneficent effect is not clear.

The usual restraint as to marriage within the gens did not exist. Individuals were free to select wives as they saw fit, so long as they were not blood relations. There was no marriage ceremony, and polygyny was common. Infidelity of wives was punished in the usual Plains Indian fashion by cutting off a portion of the nose, a disfigurement that would seem to have restrained any potentially errant woman; yet the Indian love of gambling not infrequently induced women to take chances even when their noses were at stake. During the summer of 1926 the author was in an encampment where an Indian wife lost her nose through such an indiscretion, although in this instance the inconstancy was potential rather than actual, as the woman was a participant in the [non-traditional] Forty-nine dance, ... Indian women generally are not below the average of their Caucasian sisters in chastity. In his description of the various family relationships of the Comanche, [Robert S.] Neighbors, [special agent to the Comanche,] wrote:

The ties of consanguinity are very strong, not only with regard to their blood relations, but extends itself to relations by marriage, etc., who are considered as, and generally called 'brothers'—all offences committed against any member, are avenged by all, or any member connected with the family. . . . The marriage state only continues during the pleasure of the parties, as a man claims the right to divorce himself whenever he chooses. Polygamy is practised to a great extent—some chiefs having more than ten wives, but inconstancy is the natural result of it, which is frequently punished by cutting off the nose of the transgressor, and sometimes even by death;

but more frequently the woman escapes unpunished, and the seducer is deprived of all his available property which is yielded to the injured party, by custom, without resistance.

The women perform all manual labor, war and hunting being all the occupation of the men. Jealousy is frequently a great cause of discord, but the husband exercises unbounded authority over the person of his wife. Their lodges are generally neat, and on the entrance of a stranger, the owner of a lodge designates the route he shall pass, and the seat he shall occupy. Any infringement of this rule is liable to give offense.

They are formal and suspicious to strangers, but hospitable and social to those they consider their friends. They have no regular meals, but eat when they feel hungry, each party helping himself, and joining in the meal without invitation or ceremony. The parents exercise full control in giving their daughters in marriage, they being generally purchased at a stipulated price by their suitors. There is no marriage ceremony of any description—they enter the marriage state at a very early age, frequently before the age of puberty. The children are named from some circumstance in tender years, which is frequently changed in after life by some act of greater importance. Whatever children are stolen from their enemies, are incorporated in the family to whom they belong, and treated as their own children, without distinction of color or nation. There is considerable respect shown by the younger branches of the community to the patriarchal chiefs of the tribe.

Concerning their mortuary customs, [David G.] Burnet says:

They imagine that good men (and adroitness and daring in taking scalps or stealing horses are capital evidences of goodness) are translated at death to elysian hunting-grounds, where buffalo are always abundant and fat. The reverse of this maximum of Comanche felicity is assigned to the wicked. In order to facilitate the posthumous enjoyments of a deceased warrior, they sacrifice some of his best horses, and bury in his grave his favorite implements of the chase for his future use. They have no determinate idea of the locality of these imaginary hunting-grounds. They mourn for the dead systematically and periodically with great noise and vehemence; at which times the female relatives of the deceased scarify their arms and legs with sharp flints until the blood trickles from a thousand pores. The duration of these lamentations depends on the quality and estimation of the deceased; varying from three to five or seven days: after which the curtain of oblivion seems to be drawn around the grave.

In their invocations they address 'Father Above' and 'Mother

Earth.' There is an indefinable relationship between Father Above and the Sun. The golden eagle is symbolic of the sun, in fact symbolizes the Infinite. There being such a dearth of culture legends pertaining to precepts and teachings, it is no longer possible to gain a satisfactory insight into the mental processes of the Comanche. They believe that knowledge came from the spirits and was obtained by the individual through long periods of fasting. Such knowledge included that of healing and of ceremonies, and could be transferred to others.

At the climax of their existence the Comanche were apparently divided into twelve or more bands, but through tribal disintegration this band organization is almost lost.

Each band had a chief and a second chief who were chosen by the voice of the band in council. Naturally only those noted for bravery and success in warfare were selected. As the dominating position of any band of the organization was dependent in large measure on its chief, it was most important to have as leaders men of great skill and daring. The Comanche did not have the soldier societies so characteristic of the tribal government of most Plains tribes. In his report to [H. R.] Schoolcraft, Neighbors wrote as follows in regard to Comanche chiefs:

The position of a chief is not hereditary, but the result of his own superior cunning, knowledge, or success in war, or some act or acts that rank him according to his merits. The subjects under discussion in council are at all times open to popular opinion, and the chiefs are the main exponents of it. The democratic principle is strongly implanted in them. The chiefs consult, principally, the warrior class, and the weaker minds are wholly influenced by popular opinion. War chiefs commit hostilities without consulting the other tribes. Any proposition or treaties proposed by the whites are discussed privately, and the answer given by the chief as the unanimous voice of the tribe. In deliberations in council, they consult each other, and one addresses the meeting. The council is opened by passing the council pipe from one to the other, invoking the Deity to preside. It is conducted with great propriety, and closed in the same manner. There is one appointed as crier or messenger, whose duty it is to fill the pipe, etc. Questions of importance are deliberately considered, and considerable time frequently elapses before they are answered; but they are all decided on the principle of apparent unanimity. Capital punishments are rare; each party acting generally for himself, and avenging his own injuries. Each chief is ranked according to his popularity, and his rank is maintained on the same principle. He is deprived of his office by any misfortune, such as loss of many men in battle, or even a single defeat, or being taken prisoner, but never for any private act unconnected with the welfare of the whole tribe. They have no medals except those lately given them, which are worn more as symbols of peace than as marks of distinction among themselves. The priesthood appear to exercise no influence in their general government, but, on war being declared, they exert their influence with the Deity. . . . Any principal chief has a right to call a general council of his own tribe [band], and a council of all the tribes is called by the separate chiefs of each tribe. . . . The principal chiefs have shown every disposition to advance in civilization, and only require the co-operation of the Americans, to influence their followers in the same course.

No individual action is considered as a crime, but every man acts for himself according to his own judgement, unless some superior power, for instance, that of a popular chief, should exercise authority over him. They believe that when they were created, the Great Spirit gave them the privilege of a free and unconstrained use of their individual faculties.

The dress of these nomads closely resembled that of the Plains tribes of the north, for the men dressed in deerskin shirts, leggings, and moccasins. The women wore one-piece costumes of tanned skin, and distinctive, beautifully made, knee-length boots. Indian women take great pride in their footwear, and every tribe had distinctive boots, moccasins, or moccasin-leggings. Once inquiring of a middle-age woman as to why this was so, with a twinkle in her eye she said to the writer, 'To attract the eye of man.' In the matter of dress, Neighbors wrote:

> Their [the men's] common dress is the breech-cloth and moccasins, with a buffalo robe flung loosely over the shoulders; . . . They [the Comanche generally] have a great variety of ornaments, many of which are of pure silver, principally fashioned into large brooches. Their decorations are derived from birds and shells which are bartered to them by the traders. The hawk and eagle feathers are the most esteemed of the bird. They use several native dyes, produced from roots. . . . Vermilion, indigo, and verdigris are sold them by the traders. They also paint with white and red clay on particular occasions.

The Comanche of today live on an allotted reservation in Caddo county, Oklahoma, set aside for them, as well as for the Kiowa and the Kiowa Apache, under the treaty of 1867. Their fertile lands possess splendid agricultural possibilities.

Many of the more progressive men till their lands successfully, notwithstanding the fact that before being assigned their reservation the Comanche were in no sense an agricultural tribe; but the majority prefer to lease their holdings to white settlers. The old wrinkled men, as a rule, sit about and tell of the days of their

9 *Comanche Footwear*

ancestors when life was real and full of action. And the men of all ages spend the major portion of their time, as do those of other tribes, in discussing the suits brought or contemplated against the Government on account of broken treaties.

XIX (1930), 181–188

10 The Cahuilla, a Southern Shoshoneon people, mostly live around Palm Cañon near San Jacinto Mountain, California

2 Homelands and Habitations

Home of the Havasupai

The home of the Havasupai is in Cataract Cañon, a branch of the Grand Cañon of the Colorado. Without question it is the strangest dwelling place of any tribe in America. In all the long leagues of the cañon's windings there is but one small spot where the gorge widens. Here is an amphitheatre. Its bottom has filled with earth, the weatherings of untold ages, and at the spot where the narrow rift begins to widen the blue water springs from the earth. The clean, clear cut, perpendicular walls of red sandstone tower four hundred feet toward the heavens, and back of these sheer walls are others, but broken, ragged, cut, cañoned, and tumbled into a wilderness of rock, ever mounting higher, until at the cañon's rim one is three thousand feet above the bottom of the chasm in which these people have their home. Standing on the edge and looking down into this bewildering gorge one sees many fanciful forms, fashioned through eons from the world of rock: castles, citadels, pyramids, pinnacles, and sphinx-like sculptures, tinted and mystified with the incomparable atmospheric coloring of the desert, and ever wrapped in death-like stillness. As he gazes there is nothing to suggest that half a mile below and twenty miles away, at the bottom of this awful gash, is a garden spot, and a village of humans.

To reach this little oasis there are but two trails, and he who selects one will wish he had taken the other; both follow routes chosen by prehistoric man. The sandalled feet of unknown generations toiled up and down these tortuous ways ages before there was need of making them accessible for beasts of burden. After hours of winding about sheer cliffs, down narrow gorges, patiently picking a way back and forth across crumbling rocky slopes, one reaches at last the home of the Havasupai. The floor is half a mile wide, scarcely two miles long, and contains an area of less than five hundred acres. The never-ending stream from which this small but picturesque tribe derives its name, ['Blue Water People',] and which makes life possible in the depths of the gorge, flows through the length of the little garden spot, then in a cataract leaps from the floor of the cañon to be caught in a pool below.

11 A Havasupai dwelling on the floor of the Cataract Cañon

While the brink of the cañon lies in the high plateau region, the land of the piñon, cedar, and pine, the home of the Havasupai is in almost a subtropical spot that produces luxuriant vegetation with fruits of several kinds. Ask a Havasupai whence came these fruits and vegetables, and he will tell you, 'God brought them, all but the figs.' This frank expression as to the origin of his garden products reflects a Havasupai peculiarity. Ordinarily Indians will not mention their gods by name, but the Havasupai discuss them with the same familiarity that they would their neighbors.

In 1903 the Havasupai numbered about 250, but in three years disease has diminished their population to 166. The inaccessibility of their cañon home has tended to keep them immune from outside influences, so that in many ways their life is still delightfully primitive. Their typical dwelling consists of a framework covered with brush or tule and sometimes with an outer covering of earth. In summer a four-post brush shelter is erected, which affords protection from the sun and allows free circulation of air.

The agave plant, cut and prepared in much the same way as by the Apache, has always been an important article of food among these people. Other native vegetal foods are grass seeds and piñon nuts. From time immemorial the Havasupai have been hunters.

On the approach of winter they left the cañon for the upper levels, built wickiups of boughs and bark, and spent the cold season in hunting. Deer were the principal game, although they killed some mountain sheep and an occasional black bear. Much of the venison was cut in thin strips and dried for summer use. Deerskin dressed by the Havasupai was considered the best by all neighboring tribes; consequently, it not only furnished clothing, but was an important medium of barter. But the life of the Havasupai has changed. Game is scarce, and the Government does not willingly grant them permission to hunt on the surrounding mesas, hence there is little wonder that the wrinkled veterans long for the old days when game was plentiful and they hunted where they would. 'Now all is changed,' they say. 'We cannot go out of the cañon without asking the white man. We dare not hunt deer, as the game must be saved for the [whites]. We are no longer men; we are like little children; we must always ask Washington!'

Corn is now their chief staple, besides which they raise beans, squashes, melons, pumpkins, sunflowers, peaches, apricots, and figs. They prepare corn in countless ways, corresponding largely to those of the Hopi. In fact, the modes of preparing corn by all tribes of the Southwest are much the same. Much of the crop is allowed to ripen on the stalk; this is later ground into meal on the metate. Quantities of green corn are harvested, roasted in large pits with the husks on, and hung to dry. This may be ground or simply shelled and cooked, either alone or with beans, meat, and dried squash. Like the figs, their peaches and apricots were derived from the whites, but so long ago that they are now regarded as native.

II (1908), 97–100

The Environment and Houses of the Kwakiutl

In its broadest application the term Kwakiutl is used to designate a large number of cognate tribes on the coast of British Columbia between the fiftieth and the fifty-fourth parallels, the most northerly being the Haisla at the head of Douglas channel, and the most southerly the Lekwiltok at Cape Mudge and Campbell river. Properly speaking, it is the name of a group now resident at Fort Rupert, and, more specifically, of a sub-tribe of that group. These tribes compose one branch of the so-called Wakashan linguistic family; the other consisting of the Nootka tribes on the western coast of Vancouver island south of Cape Cook, and about Cape Flattery in the State of Washington.

In the south the Kwakiutl come in contact with the Salish of Vancouver island and the mainland north of Fraser river, while farther north an isolated Salish group, the Bellacoola, juts down to salt water in the midst of Kwakiutl territory, occupying Dean channel and Bentinck arm. In the extreme north the Kwakiutl are neighbors of the Tsimshian tribes and of the Haida of Queen

Charlotte islands. Intercourse with the inland Athapascan tribes is prevented by mountain barriers.

The physical characteristics of the region are remarkable. Innumerable fiords cut deeply into the mainland. For the greater part their shores are steep and rocky, even mountainous; but here and there, usually at the mouth of a stream, is enough low, level land for a village site. In the fiords and off the mainland coast are countless islands, all rocky and clothed in evergreen forests, and separated by narrow, intricate channels of deep, clear water. On such islands are many of the Kwakiutl villages. Close to the mainland, from northwest to southeast, Vancouver island stretches its two-hundred-mile length, protecting the smaller islands from heavy storms and rendering the channels safe for canoes. North of this sheltering land mass the winds from the open Pacific sweep unchecked into Queen Charlotte sound and up into Hecate strait, but the natives find safe passage in the narrow waterways behind the small islands that skirt the shore. Less fortunate are those about the unsheltered northern end of Vancouver island, who in rough weather must either remain ashore or restrict their movements to the quiet waters of their home bay or inlet. On the mainland, as on Vancouver island, the mountains come close to the sea, and with few exceptions the inhabitants are inevitably marine people.

It is an inhospitable country, with its forbidding, rock-bound coasts, its dark, tangled, mysterious forests, its beetling mountains, its long, gloomy season of rains and fogs. No less inhospitable, mysterious, and gloomy, to the casual observer, is the character of the inhabitants. They seem constantly lost in dark broodings, and it is only after long acquaintance and the rather tedious process of gaining their confidence that one discovers an uncertain thread of cheerfulness interwoven in the sombre fabric of their nature. Even then one is impelled to question their knowledge of any such thing as spiritual exaltation or mental pleasure except such as may be aroused by the gratification of savage passions or purely physical instincts. Chastity, genuine, self-sacrificing friendship, even the inviolability of a guest,—a cardinal principle among most Indian tribes,—are unknown. It is scarcely exaggeration to say that no single noble trait redeems the Kwakiutl character.

The superstructure of a Kwakiutl house is supported by heavy cedar posts. In the notched tops of the hewn side posts, usually six in number, rest two eaves-timbers extending from the rear to the front. Another hewn post supports the ends of the gable timbers in the rear wall, and two others perform a similar service at the sides of the door in the front wall. The eaves-timbers are a handbreadth in thickness and about twenty inches in width. The front end of the ridge-timber rests on a heavy cross-piece connecting the tops of two massive columns, while the rear end is supported directly by a single post. These three interior posts stand well inside the front and rear lines of the house. From ridge to eaves extend numerous rafters, which are crossed by a series of battens. The roof-boards extend in the direction of the rafters, and formerly were slightly guttered and applied like tile. They are held down only by their own weight, or, in stormy weather, by the addition of heavy stones; being left unfastened in order that they may easily be removed by means of a pole to permit the escape of smoke.

The lower ends of the perpendicular wall-boards are set in a trench, the tops in a groove in the lower edge of the eaves-timber. Formerly they were rived from large cedar logs, and it is still easy to find houses consisting almost entirely of native-made boards. They are now held in place by nails, but the primitive means were cedar withes passing through holes in the boards and binding them to horizontal battens. The poorer class laid the wall-boards horizontally and secured them with cedar withes between pairs of upright poles. Not a few houses are now constructed throughout of mill lumber.

A striking feature of almost every building of the old style is

the grotesque carving of the interior posts to represent mythical
beasts and birds. As late as 1865 houses with carved posts were by
no means numerous, and the original of each was believed to
have been given by some supernatural being to an ancient
ancestor of the family. Carved posts have become increasingly
common, the authority to make use of some certain house-frame
being one of the most valued rights transferred in marriage.

Many of the modern houses of primitive type have huge
dimensions, considering the status of the builders. In the un-
finished house at Nukapnkyim at Fort Rupert the corner posts
are forty inches thick, twenty feet high, twenty-one feet apart
laterally, and seventy-seven feet from front to rear. The eaves-
timbers are three feet thick at the butts, which rest on the rear
posts, and eighty-five feet long, projecting considerably beyond
the corner posts. Until the middle of the nineteenth century
Kwakiutl houses were very much smaller than this, the largest
not exceeding perhaps thirty feet in depth and width, six or seven
feet in height at the eaves, and nine feet at the ridge; while the
seven upright posts were not more than twelve inches in diameter.
The ponderous roof-timbers of today are raised by means of a
cribwork of logs gradually built up beneath the balanced beam.

13 A Kwakiutl House Frame

35

The principal door is in the middle of the front wall, a smaller one opening through the rear directly upon the adjacent forest.

All about the room extends a low platform of earth covered with boards, on which the guests sit. The house is apportioned among several related families, each of which maintains its own fire and kitchen devices. Beside each fire is a massive settee resting flat on the earthen floor, its sloping back bearing carved representations of fabulous creatures. The position of honor, as in the Plains tipi, is at the back of the room behind the principal fire. In the fantastically figurative thought of the Kwakiutl the house is represented as a face with the door a great mouth ready to swallow the guests of the master.

[Timber for houses and other wooden objects was aquired in a number of ways. For example,] one [sometimes] finds in the dense forest a standing cedar from which generations ago boards have been split up to the heart, leaving only half the trunk. This was accomplished by two artisans, one who made the cut at the bottom and another who worked above the ground, supported by a climbing apparatus. This device is still used by gatherers of hemlock bast. Two strong ropes encircle tree and climber, one of them passing beneath his armpits and the other about his thighs, while a third holds against the rough bark a stout stick. His feet resting on the stick, the climber slowly works the ropes upward with a short pole and lifts himself to any desired height beneath the first branch. When he is ready to descend, he throws over the lowest branch the end of the rope by which he has drawn up his implements, lowers it to his companion, ties the other end beneath his arms, casts loose the other ropes, and is then lowered to the ground. Probably the Kwakiutl resorted to this method of obtaining boards when only a few were required, and a large portion of the labor of felling a tree and cutting off a log would have been wasted.

A standing tree from which boards have been split is called ... 'begged from', and it is said that, since trees are believed to have sentient life, the ancients before obtaining boards in this way would look upward to the tree and say: 'We have come to beg a piece of you today. Please! We hope you will let us have a piece of you.' The same request was made of a yew tree before cutting off a piece for making tools. But when a tree was to be cut down, it was 'killed' without words.

X(1915), 3–4, 6–8, 11

Staple Foods of the Mono Homeland

The habitat of the Mono, who number about fifteen hundred, is in east-central California, including all of Mono county and Inyo county as far south as Owens lake. On the west are the towering snow-covered peaks of the Sierra Nevada, beyond which colonies of the Mono have established themselves in Madera and Fresno counties. These western Mono have assimilated much of the typical culture of central California.

The Mono country is far from being the desert it is often imagined to be. The rainfall, to be sure, is scanty, and districts directly dependent on the clouds are barren wastes of sand, volcanic ash, naked mountain ranges, and cinder cones. But it is south of their territory that such conditions become the rule. Most of the Mono area is near enough to the Sierra Nevada to receive unfailing streams from the snowy heights, and it would be difficult to find a more pleasing landscape than is presented in the series of valleys from Owens lake northward to the Nevada line—Big Pine, Independence, Lone Pine, Bishop, Round valley, Long valley, Mono lake, and the charming headwaters of Walker river.

Not an acre of this region drains into the sea. The extreme northern part is tributary, through Walker river, to Walker lake in Nevada. A small portion of the northern section lies above Mono lake, but far the greater part of the area drains through Owens river into Owens lake. The three lakes are salt. Strikingly symmetrical volcanic cones rise above the surface of Mono, recalling the aspect of Pyramid lake in Nevada.

The forestation of the mountains is prevailingly coniferous, and the piñons furnished a very important food staple. Alders, cotton-woods, and willows grow along the streams. Oaks do not occur here, and the Mono made regular visits to the Miwok and western Mono beyond the mountains, to secure acorns by purchase. John Muir, mounting the western side of Mono pass in 1869, met a band of them on their annual pilgrimage to Yosemite valley. His habit of viewing everything in terms of animals, trees, rocks, and glaciers gives the account an amusing turn.

> As I entered the pass . . . a drove of gray hairy beings came in sight, lumbering toward me with a kind of boneless, wallowing motion like bears. . . . I soon discovered that although as hairy as bears and as crooked as summit pines, the strange creatures were . . . nothing more formidable than Mono Indians dressed in the skins of sage-rabbits. . . . I afterward learned that they were on their way to Yosemite Valley to feast awhile on trout and procure a load of acorns to carry back through the pass to their huts on the shore of Mono Lake. . . . These . . . were mostly ugly, and some of them altogether hideous. The dirt on their faces was fairly stratified, and seemed so ancient and so undisturbed it might almost possess a geological significance.

With the advent of spring the Mono abandoned their winter houses, or even demolished them with the intention of rebuilding in another place in the fall, and began to wander about the country in quest of food. The most important vegetal foods were

14 *A Mono Home*

pine-nuts and the seeds of various grasses and Compositæ. The harvesting of pine-nuts was the principal business of the autumn. The entire band moved in a body to a favorable locality, and every member of the family engaged in the labor, men and boys swarming into the trees or knocking off the cones with long poles, and women and girls gathering them in great piles. If the cones were ripe, the nuts could be removed without further ado; but most of them were gathered green in order to forestall the busy squirrels and jays, and consequently had to be roasted in pits until the scales opened and exposed the seeds, one beneath each scale. Then all gathered around to pick out the nuts, and after appetites sharpened by months of expectation had been satisfied, the work of accumulating the winter stores proceeded. At such times the pine groves were scenes of intense animation and industry.

The bunch-grasses, wild oats, the tarweeds, and sunflowers were important sources of edible seeds, which, parched in the harvesting, were ground with metate and muller and eaten without further preparation.

The Mono are still very fond of *kuzavi*, the larval form of a small fly. The larvæ hatch under water, rise to the surface and are

38

blown ashore in enormous quantities, where they are swept into baskets by means of a besom. For the time being they are piled on the ground, and later are spread out to dry, after which they are rolled in the hands and passed through a basketry sieve in order to separate the edible portion from the enveloping tissue. Many Caucasians testify to the palatableness of the larvæ, which the Mono however mix with a kind of thick soup made of pine-nuts. Mono lake is so noted for its yield of these larvæ that its people . . . are known to the Nevada Paviotso as 'kuzavi eaters.'

XV(1926), 55–56, 62, 61–62

The Nomadic Life of the Apsaroke (or Crows)

The country which the Apsaroke ranged and claimed as their own was an extensive one for so small a tribe. In area it may be compared, east and west, to the distance from Boston to Buffalo, and north to south, from Montreal to Washington—certainly a vast region to be dominated by a tribe never numbering more than fifteen hundred warriors. The borders of their range were, roughly, a line extending from the mouth of the Yellowstone southward through the Black Hills, thence westward to the crest of the Wind River mountains, northwestward through the Yellowstone Park to the site of Helena, thence to the junction of the Musselshell and the Missouri, and down the latter stream to the mouth of the Yellowstone. This region is the veritable Eden of the Northwest. With beautiful broad valleys and abundant wooded streams, no part of the country was more favorable for buffalo, while its wild forested mountains made it almost unequalled for elk and other highland game.

In the old times the Apsaroke, during a large part of the year, were constantly on the move. One day they would be quietly encamped on one of their favorite streams, the next travelling away in quest of buffalo or solely for the mere pleasure of going. Their customary camps were along the mountain streams, where the lodges were commonly placed in a circle, but at times, where the valley was narrow, they were close together, parallel-ing the wooded watercourse.

The larger camps were always the scene of great activity. Horses were tethered everywhere close at hand; on the slopes far and near thousands were grazing, while on the nearby hilltops groups of people were statuesquely outlined against the sky. Here are chiefs and councillors in quiet discussion of tribal affairs. As they pass the pipe from man to man and look down upon the village with its hundreds of lodges their eyes are glad, for the picture is one of plenty, and the murmur of the camp as it is wafted to their ears tells of happiness. Close by are laughing, romping children, the bronze skin of their rounded bodies gleaming in the sunlight, and the old men reflect, 'It is well that their bodies know the heat and the cold; it will make them strong warriors and mothers.' On another hill proud youths are seen, decked in the savage trappings that make glad their hearts. Their words are of the hunt, the war-path, and sweethearts. Not far distant is a group of maidens gayly dressed in garments of soft skins. It is not many moons since they romped about with the freedom of fawns, unabashed that the breeze caressed their bodies; but all that is past now; they are maidens, every part save face and hands must be carefully concealed, and a keen-eyed mother is always near. But all cannot be childhood and youth and love-making; on other outlooks are wrinkled old women who live only in the past, muttering and dreaming of the days of their youth, when husbands and sweethearts rode away to conflict,—of the days when brave warriors stole them from the arms of others,—when warrior husbands took them along on their forays, perhaps to see their men killed and themselves borne off by the victorious Lakota, on whose coup-sticks waved the hair upon which they had lavished so much loving attention. Farther from the village mourners cry out in anguish for those whose lives have been taken; and on distant peaks are lonely men fasting through the long days and nights in supplication for spiritual strength.

In the camp itself there is an endless panorama of activities and a ceaseless confusion of sounds. Women are everywhere stretching the drying hides, and filling great drying-racks with long thin strips of rich, red buffalo-meat. In the lodges others are tanning skins, and on many sides can be heard the thud of the wooden tray as women gamble with plum-seed dice. In other lodges men are shouting a wild song as they engage in the hand gambling game, while in the open another group is playing at hoop-and-pole, and others the game of the arrows. The sick and the wounded are being cared for by medicine-men, who accompany their incantation with rattle and drum. Men and women, old and young, are constantly passing from lodge to lodge for a word or a smoke, and food is always placed before them.

As evening approaches the people begin to gather around the lodge-fires, and with the arrival of men laden with the product of the hunt, the village assumes an even livelier air. Heralds of the chiefs are shouting invitations to the feasts, and as night falls the lodges glow in the darkness. If the weather is at all cool, the evening is spent mostly indoors, where on soft skins and furs heaped in profusion the people lounge in full contentment. From many dwellings echo the muffled beat of the drum and the droning song of men and women, and occasionally is heard the doleful note of a flute as some lovesick youth serenades his sweetheart.

Early in the morning the village is astir, for the counsel of the men who have thoughts is, 'Do not follow the sleep to the end, but waken when it requires determination; be up and alive to what is going on about you!' As soon as the family awaken they throw blankets around their bodies and go to the river for their morning bath. If the water is icy cold, so much the better, for it requires a strong heart to plunge in, and it inures the body to cold and heat. Husband and wife and small children go together, each family a group of itself. Probably not ten yards away is another family, and so on for a mile or more, many hundreds bathing at the same time. At other hours of the day it would be the height of impropriety for a woman to expose any part of her body, but at the morning bath there is no embarrassment, 'for this is our custom,' they say. Truly custom is a strange thing, for an Apsaroke woman—who a half-hour before had been playing about in the water like a happy seal—blushes at the picture of a white woman in a décolleté gown, and says, 'Such women have no shame!' Parties of maidens, accompanied by some watchful mother, bathe in secluded nooks.

When the chief decides that camp is to be moved, his herald goes through the village in the evening, crying out, 'Prepare, prepare! To-morrow we move!' And again at the first blush of day he rides from end to end of the village, calling '. . . To-day the chief says we move toward the buffalo! Men, bring in the horses; women, throw down the lodges!' As all have known from the previous announcement that they are to move, the morning meal is finished before daylight appears. Soon all the herds of horses come trotting in and the women are running about among them throwing ropes over the necks of the old, gentle pack-animals. Others are at work on the lodges, the covers of which come rattling down, soon making of the camp a skeleton of bare poles. From the middle of each framework a column of smoke curls skyward; sleepy children still in their blankets are rolled out as their mothers pull the robes from under them in the work of packing. The tousled-headed young- sters whimper for something to eat and are thrown a hard, dry piece of meat for their breakfast. Soon the horses are packed with high bundles of robes and clothing, and the lodge-poles tied at the sides, usually six to a side, two horses being required for each lodge. Here and there horses break away and go galloping through the camp before their packs are secured, scattering their loads broadcast, and causing great excitement and confusion. Women call, children cry, grandmothers chatter and mumble.

The chief rides off a short distance in the direction they are to go, and some of his old men sit about him smoking and talking. Then they move forward a distance and halt while the people complete their preparations for the march. Now the line begins to form—first the chiefs and old men; then a band of arrogant, gayly dressed Lumpwoods, with newly stolen wives riding behind and carrying their husbands' shields and lances; next a body of clansmen with a group of proud young wives bedecked in all their finery. Behind them the column continues to form, family by family, each driving its herd of horses, until at length

15 A storm brews above a Flathead camp on the Jocko River

come straggling by those who have been slow in packing. A moving column of six hundred lodges is miles in length and of a width determined by the groups of families or by the nature of the country traversed. When they near the place the chief has designated for the night's camp, many of the grandfathers ride ahead and select spots for their own lodges, clear the ground, and gather dry wood. As the irregular line drags in, they stand beside their chosen places, calling out to their wives where to come. If the weather be cold, they already have kindled small fires, and now take down the little children from the tops of the packs and hold them in the warmth of the leaping flames.

A splendid picture of the nomad's life they made as the caravan moved across far-reaching plain, hill, and valley. The crossing of a broad stream added much to the animation of the scene. One summer nine hundred and fifty lodges of Apsaroke went to the Yellowstone, intending to cross. As the water was very high and the river nearly half a mile in width, the Kick Bellys, numbering four hundred and fifty lodges, lost their courage, and would not attempt the crossing. All the others, however, were unafraid and passed over. They used no boats, but made small rafts of driftwood, laying the ends of the lodge-poles on these rude craft, and allowing the tops to float on the water behind. On the poles a large piece of old lodge-covering was spread, and on that were piled the domestic belongings, the edges of the skin being gathered up and tied at the top to protect the load from splashing water. Perched upon this bundle rode the old women and the children. Two young men grasped the manes of strong swimming horses and swam along by their side, towing the raft across. Behind, holding to the ends of the lodge-poles, swam the young women and maidens, clad only in a short skirt reaching from waist to knee. It was a time of great merriment and fun-making, yet one not without its serious side, for a tottering old woman gazed long at the swirling river and, declaring that she was not afraid to die but feared the water, stabbed herself and fell lifeless. The crossing occupied four days, for the current was swift, and many who had no horses were compelled to wait for assistance from their relatives. Before going into the water men and women painted red stripes about waist, wrists, and ankles, for protection against the water-monsters that were believed to inhabit all large streams. Necklaces of white beads were never worn in the water, for beads of that sort were believed to be hailstones, the symbol of the Thunderbird, a deadly enemy of water-monsters, which therefore would be glad to swallow any one thus showing his friendship with the Thunderbird.

IV(1909), 4–8

Hopi Homeland

Since they first appeared in history in the sixteenth century, these Indians have occupied their present habitat in northeastern Arizona. Their neighbors on the north, west, and east were the predatory Navaho, alternately hostile and friendly, now raiding the Hopi fields and sheep ranges, now visiting the pueblo festivals, sometimes even receiving Hopi migrants and marrying them. From the north and east came also the warlike Ute, to combat whom the Hopi more than once called in Tewa settlers from the distant Rio Grande. Southward the country was overrun by nomadic bands of Apache, who frequently swooped down from the mountains south and west of the present Winslow. About a hundred miles to the southeast were the Zuñi villages, the romantic Seven Cities of Cibola of the Spanish adventurers; and beyond them to the Rio Grande, and particularly along that stream, were numerous pueblos, with all of which the Hopi held more or less intercourse. Far to the west, in and about the Grand cañon, were the Havasupai and Walapai, both of the Yuman stock, whom Hopi traders regularly visited for the purpose of exchanging yarn and blankets for deerskins, and who in turn annually brought roasted mescal and piñon-nuts to the Hopi.

The reservation of 3863 square miles lies in the eastern watershed of the Little Colorado, but at no point does it extend to the

43

16 *Walpi*, a picturesque Hopi pueblo

river. In fact there is no perennial stream within its borders. The country is typical of the semi-arid Southwest. Broad sandy wastes are broken by rocky buttes and fantastically eroded mesas rising abruptly from the general level. Some seventy-five miles to the southwest the San Francisco mountains are visible, snow-covered in winter. High temperature prevails during the days of summer, but the nights are refreshingly cool. As the country lies at an elevation of about six thousand five hundred feet, the winter nights are fairly rigorous, but delightful, sunny days are the rule. A more healthful climate it would be difficult to find, and the harmonious pastel shades of sand, rock, and vegetation, the huge, cottony billows that float aloft on a summer's after-noon, the glorious cloud effects at sunset, the distant ranges of lavender mountains slowly transformed into turquois as the lowering sun sinks behind them, the incredible blueness of the sky and brilliance of the stars, take hold of the heart and call one back again and again.

Considerable moisture is stored in the soil by snowfall, and the frequent heavy rains of midsummer, coursing down the slopes toward the washes, are guided into the cultivated fields and suffice for the deep-rooted Hopi corn and beans.

The vegetation is characteristically desert. Sage and greasewood dot the sand in clumps, and the latter furnishes the bulk of the fuel. The principal trees are the juniper and the piñon, the latter yielding edible nuts and house timbers. The distant mountains are clothed with coniferous forests, in which pines predominate, but these were of little concern to the Hopi except at the period of the Spanish missionaries, when the padres induced them to transport on their backs pine beams from San Francisco mountains.

The fauna of the Hopi country and the immediately surrounding region included antelope, deer, elk, mountain-sheep, cougar, wolf, coyote, fox, wildcat, bear (both *Americanus* and *horribilis*), beaver, porcupine, badger, cotton-tail and jack-rabbit, condor, eagle, buzzard, various hawks and waterfowl, and wild turkey.

There are now eight Hopi pueblos, all of them on the tops of mesas. On East mesa are Walpi . . . ('gap place') and Sichomovi . . . ('flower mound place'); on Middle mesa, Mishongnovi . . . Shipaulovi . . . and Shongopavi . . . ('rush spring place'); on West mesa, Oraibi . . . Hotavila . . . ('juniperwood slope'), and Pakavi . . . ('reed place'). Hotavila and Pakavi were established

17 *The North Pueblo at Taos*, a Tiwa settlement in New Mexico

only within the last few years by dissatisfied factions from Oraibi. At East mesa also is Hano . . . a Tewa pueblo founded early in the eighteenth century by emigrants from the Rio Grande.

XII(1922), 4–6

18 *A Paguate Entrance* in this village of the Laguna Keres in New Mexico

3 Historical Sketches

The Spaniards arrive at Acoma

The Keres village of Acoma is the oldest continuously occupied settlement in the United States. Perched on the top of a mesa some three hundred and fifty feet above the surrounding valley, accessible by difficult trails partly cut in the solid rock of its precipices, it is no less picturesquely placed than Walpi.

Under the name Acus it was first mentioned by Friar Marcos de Niza, discoverer of the Zuñi towns. He did not visit the place, but in the following year, 1540, Coronado sent one of his officers from Cibola to explore the country eastward. [G. P. Winship writes as follows:]

> Captain Alvarado started on this journey and in five days reached a village which was on a rock called Acuco [Acoma] having a population of about 200 men. These people were robbers, feared by the whole country round about. The village was very strong, because it was up on a rock out of reach, having steep sides in every direction, and so high that it was a very good musket that could throw a ball as high. There was only one entrance by a stairway built by hand, which began at the top of a slope which is around the foot of the rock. There was a broad stairway for about 200 steps, then a stretch of about 100 narrower steps, and at the top they had to go up about three times as high as a man by means of holes in the rock, in which they put the points of their feet, holding on at the same time by their hands. There was a wall of large and small stones at the top, which they could roll down without showing themselves, so that no army could possibly be strong enough to capture the village. On the top they had room to sow and store a large amount of corn, and cisterns to collect snow and water. These people came down to the plain ready to fight, and would not listen to any arguments. They drew lines on the ground and determined to prevent our men from crossing these, but when they saw that they would have to fight they offered to make peace before any harm had been done. They went through their forms of making peace, which is to touch the horses and take their sweat and rub themselves

with it, and to make crosses with the fingers of the hands.
But to make the most secure peace they put their hands across
each other, and they keep this peace inviolably.

In 1598 Juan de Zaldívar, one of Oñate's captains, was attacked
by the warriors of Acoma, and about half of his force of thirty
men, including the leader himself, were killed. A month later,
in January, 1599, Vicente de Zaldívar with seventy men attacked
the stronghold and in a three-day siege and assault avenged his
brother by slaying, it is said, half of its three thousand inhabitants.
Although Fray Gerónimo de Zárate Salmerón, who reached
New Mexico about 1617, served as missionary to Acoma, the
first fraile to become permanently established there was Fray
Juan Ramírez, one of the band of Franciscans who accompanied
Fray Estevan Perea in 1629. His reception was not of the most

48

hospitable nature, for he was greeted with a shower of arrows. It chanced however that a little girl fell from the cliff, landing unhurt near the Father, who bore her to the summit and restored her to her people, who believed that she had been killed. After this apparent miracle Fray Juan was favorably received. He remained in Acoma many years, erecting a church and building a trail which horses could ascend. This church was doubtless destroyed in the revolt of 1680, when the Acoma murdered their priest, for which they went unpunished.

They fared little worse after the minor outbreak of 1696, in which year [Don Diego de] Vargas destroyed some of their growing corn and captured five men. There was no way to take the village from the rear, as he had done with the Cochiti at Potrero Viejo and with the Jemez on their heights, and he was too prudent to attempt a direct assault of the position. Besides, there was wanting the personal element that inspired Vicente de Zaldívar.

As if in bitter memory of the experience with the two Zaldí- 20 *The Old Trail at Acoma*

vars, Acoma has always been one of the least tractable pueblos. Visitors used to be tolerated if they made their stay brief, but it was impossible to learn much about their practices. Severe corporal punishment was inflicted upon such of the younger generation as tried to avoid or slight their religious duties, which included bowing to the absolute will of the cacique and his fellows, and contributing to the support of that priest and the shamans. And of course it was well understood that revelations of any sort would call for measures even more drastic.

XVI(1926), 169–172

The Final Suppression of the Cheyenne

[From about the time of the Fort Laramie Treaty of September, 1851, when Indian possession of certain territories was supposedly acknowledged, there was constant friction between the Cheyenne and the US government, the worst incidents happening in the 1860s.]

In April, 1864, there occurred a fight between the Cheyenne and troops—the first active demonstration against the army since 1857. During the following summer the Cheyenne committed many depredations and had several slight brushes with small bodies of soldiers. On November 29, 1864, occurred the Chivington affair in Colorado. Many of the conflicts with our Indian tribes make dark pages in the shameful record of a civilized and superior people's subjection of a weaker race, but this butchery of the Cheyenne at Sand Creek will always stand without a parallel. Perhaps the only slaughter of Indians that can be compared with it is that occurring at Camp Grant, Arizona, in April, 1871, when a band of Arivaipa Apache, under Government protection, were set upon by a horde of Americans, Mexicans, and Papago, and murdered, neither women nor children being spared. This disgraceful massacre was the work of a mob, while that at Sand Creek was committed by troops under the command of officers.

A calm, dispassionate view of the affair—if one can dispassionately consider it—shows conclusively that the five hundred Cheyenne at the Sand Creek camp were there at the solicitation of the Government, and under its protection; and that while these people were encamped at a place designated by the Government, Colorado troops to the number of about a thousand, under the command of Colonel J. M. Chivington, attacked them at daylight, while there floated over Chief Black Kettle's lodge a United States flag and a white one on the same pole. It is certain that Chivington knew of the status of this band, that he had been begged by men in his own command not to attack friendly Indians, and that previous to the attack, and while presumably free from excitement, he ordered his men to kill large and small, men and women, particularly insisting that no prisoners were wanted; and there can be no question that he and the officers under him had full knowledge of the barbarities of the massacre. It is no less certain that the majority of the Indians in the camp were women and children, and that only about one-third of those killed were mature men, or warriors. The evidence is likewise conclusive that practically all of those killed were scalped; that women as well as men were so mutilated as to render description unprintable; that in at least one instance a woman was ripped open and her unborn child thrown by her side; that defenceless women, exposing their breasts to show their sex, and begging for mercy, were shot down with revolvers placed practically against the flesh; that hours after the attack, when there was not a militant Indian within miles of the camp, children were used as targets. Unparalleled as were the atrocities of the first day, the participants in them had at least the excuse of excitement, but there is not even that apology for the events of the second day, when soldiers turned ghouls and prowled about the devastated camp ground, searching out bodies to scalp and mutilate. From some hiding-place a toddling, naked infant appeared on this second day's scene of death, and soldiers vied with one another in shooting at it. Not satisfied with the savagery of the battle-field, the returned troops had their own form of scalp-dance by attending *en masse* a theatrical performance in an opera house at Denver, and there brandishing some fifty of the freshly taken scalps. It is doubtful if a like reversion to barbarism can be found in the history of the last few centuries.

The Sand Creek affair, as an object lesson, probably did strike terror into the hearts of the Cheyenne, both friendly and hostile; but rather than deterring them from further hostility, it naturally whetted their desire for revenge, and for a few months the white population of the region paid dearly for this inhumanity, [and the war continued, with similar ferocity and futility for more than a decade, and included many major battles.]

The seventeen years of conflict with the Cheyenne, costing hundreds of lives of both civilians and soldiers, as well as untold millions in funds, were unquestionably directly or indirectly of our own making, through the unfortunate but apparently inevitable disregard of the Indians' rights. Half the money spent in waging war would have saved, in the hands of capable humane executives possessing a knowledge of Indians, practically all bloodshed and carried the tribes through this trying period of transformation from the freest of nomadic hunters to reservation dependents, accepting the sad change pathetically but without conflict. Secretary of the Interior O. H. Browning, in his report for 1868, states: 'It is believed that peaceful relations would have been maintained to this hour had Congress, in accordance with the estimates submitted, made the necessary appropriations to enable this department to perform engagements for which the public faith was pledged. A costly Indian war, with all its horrors, would have been avoided.' Mr. N. G. Taylor, Commissioner of

Indian Affairs and member of the Peace Commission, estimated the awful cost as twenty-four lives and a million dollars for every Indian killed during this period.

In these years of Cheyenne and Arapaho conflict, the Northern Cheyenne played but a secondary part, having allied themselves with the Sioux, particularly Red Cloud's Ogalala. Indeed, so close was the alliance that these Cheyenne joined the Sioux in the Black Hills council of September 20, 1875. The cry of 'gold in the Black Hills' had gone out, prospectors and miners were flocking into the country without regard to the existing treaty with the Sioux, and in 1875 a commission was sent for the purpose of securing a relinquishment of the Black Hills portion of the reservation, or the privilege of mining for a term of years. The Indians were arrogant in demeanor and so exorbitant in their desires (making the demand that they be supported without effort on their part for seven generations) that no arrangements could be consummated.

Following their participation in this abortive council, the Cheyenne took an important part in the Sioux hostilities, growing out of encroachment by whites on the Black Hills territory. By the end of the year 1875 the situation was so menacing, and the minor depredations of the Indians were so numerous, that serious plans were inaugurated toward sending a strong force into the field against them. General [George] Crook, commanding the Department of the Platte, was instructed to make a winter campaign against the hostiles. The first conflict occurred on March seventeenth, when General J. J. Reynolds, with parts of the Second and Third Infantry, and half-breed scouts, engaged a party consisting largely of Cheyenne but under Crazy Horse, an Ogalala, while encamped on Little Powder river, Montana. The charge was made at daylight, the camp taken with the first impetuous rush, and lodges, camp equipment, and ammunition were destroyed at once. The Indians soon rallied, and opened an annoying fire on the troops, who were also suffering fearfully from the cold, many being badly frozen. Notwithstanding the apparent success of the attack, the order, for some inexplicable reason, was quickly given to abandon the field. This was done with such haste that the dead were left in the hands of the Indians. This was the one effort of the winter campaign, and the failure to do more than to destroy the camp and capture a few worthless horses was a keen disappointment to the army.

On June 17, 1876, General Crook's command, consisting of the Second and Third Cavalry and the Fourth and Ninth Infantry, and some two hundred and fifty Crow and Shoshoni scouts, met the main force of the hostiles in the hills west of Rosebud river, Montana. The battle was a severe one from the start, and judging from the testimony of Sioux and Cheyenne participants, as well as the Crow allies of the army, had it not been for the Crow and Shoshoni scouts, Crook would have received severe punishment if not defeat. He buried his dead on the battle-field, and on the following day started on his return to the commissary camp, which he had left on Goose creek, a small tributary to Tongue river.

Immediately following this, [General G. A.] Custer, with the Seventh Cavalry, came up the Rosebud almost to the scene of Crook's battle, then crossed the divide between the Rosebud and the Little Bighorn, and on the twenty-fifth, seven days after the Crook affair, and about twelve miles from its scene, occurred the Custer engagement. While this is considered a conflict with the Sioux, the Northern Cheyenne were largely represented, and apparently considered the Sioux cause their own.

On November twenty-fifth Colonel [R. S.] Mackenzie, with nearly two thousand troops, including his Indian scouts, engaged the Cheyenne on Crazy Woman creek, Wyoming. The attack was made at daylight, and was a complete surprise. Men, women, and children rushed from their beds practically without clothing, and the troops, vastly outnumbering the Indians, quickly drove them from the camp. The weather was so severe that the soldiers, bundled in all the clothing they could get on their bodies, suffered seriously, but what the misery of the almost naked Indians must have been is beyond conjecture. Many children were frozen to death during the day. After the first stampede from the camp the Indians rallied and continued a stubborn fight during the entire day. The lodges and their contents were burned, and frightful must have been the rage of the freezing Cheyenne as they beheld the destruction of their warm blankets and clothing, their lodges and ammunition. This was the worst defeat suffered by the Cheyenne.

The disheartened Dull Knife at once went for aid to his old-time comrade in conflict, Crazy Horse, but the latter would not succor him, nor aid him in a battle of retaliation. This further discouragement caused Dull Knife to surrender and offer to join the troops in a fight against the now despised Sioux chief, and early in the year 1877 practically all of his band had come in to Red Cloud agency and surrendered.

During the autumn of 1876 Colonel (General) Nelson A. Miles had been persistently campaigning against the northern Teton Sioux under Sitting Bull and Gall, and on January 8, 1877, he met Crazy Horse in the Wolf mountains of Montana. The battle-ground was of the chief's choosing, but notwithstanding his confidence and the strength of his position, he was soon dis-lodged and driven from the field. Perhaps with this crushing defeat Crazy Horse realized his mistake in not supporting Dull Knife with his large following of freezing Cheyenne. Realizing the futility of further resistance, the greatest of the Sioux chiefs, with his whole following and such Cheyenne as were with him, came in and surrendered.

Practically the only band still unconquered was that led by Lame Deer, who thought that by keeping well within the fastnesses of the mountains and the wilds he could avoid disastrous conflict with the troops. It fell to the lot of Colonel Miles to give chase to this last hostile Cheyenne band. With his command he left his cantonment at Tongue River, May 1, 1877, and moved with all possible stealth in the hope of surprising Lame Deer's camp, which was supposedly on the Little Muddy, now Lamedeer creek. In this he was successful, surprising the camp at sunrise on the sixth of May and capturing it with slight loss to the troops. As the result of the ill-considered act of a thoughtless orderly in covering Lame Deer with his rifle, the chief was tragically killed while shaking hands with Colonel Miles, and at the same instant a shot was fired at the officer, who with quick intuition dodged and saved his life.

The battle of the Little Muddy was the closing conflict in the three years' warfare with the Northern Cheyenne. The final result of the campaign was that a large part of the Cheyenne were taken to Indian Territory in the summer of 1877. Captivity in a humid climate did not agree with these men of the north, and as their numbers lessened from disease and discouragement their longing for the old home increased, and on September 9, 1878, Dull Knife and about three hundred of his people broke away and started northward. Their path was a scene of bloodshed and outrage, and notwithstanding their insignificant numbers and the vigor of the campaign against them, they succeeded in reaching Dakota. With troops increased by reënforcements and further strengthened by Indian scouts, the pursuit of the fugitive Cheyenne was continued into the wilds of Dakota, where, on October twenty-third, Dull Knife and his band were captured. Little Wolf with a small company escaped. The prisoners were taken to Fort Robinson, Nebraska, and thrown into an old barrack. Notwithstanding their continual protest against being taken to the unhealthful south, they were notified in January that they were to be taken back. Against this ultimatum Wild Hog, in a characteristic speech in behalf of the tribe, protested and expressed the determination to die there fighting rather than to be taken south to die of disease. That such a determination meant almost certain death must have been apparent to them. They numbered at that time but forty-nine men and ninety-nine women and children.

Following Wild Hog's defiant protest an effort was made to starve and freeze the captives into submission. No food or fuel was given them for five days, and for three days the water supply was withheld. At the end of that time the officers induced Wild Hog to come out for a parley, and an effort was at once made to arrest him. He fought like a madman, but in the end was manacled. This act of treachery further embittered the Indians,

21 *Little Wolf*, a chief who survived the final suppression of the Cheyenne

who at once covered the windows of their prison, and in conceal-ment tore up the floor for use as a barricade. During the night of January 10, 1879, the Indians, having secretly retained possession of three guns, shot the guards and began a desperate but hopeless effort for freedom. They were pursued by the troops and shot down wherever one could be found. More than thirty were killed that night. The final struggle of the remnant of the band occurred on January twenty-second, when, although surrounded by four companies of cavalry, nineteen warriors with their women and children once more, true to the words of Wild Hog, refused to surrender. In the charge that quickly followed twenty-three were killed, fewer than fifteen making their escape and joining Little Wolf. On March twenty-fifth that chief and the remnant of the Northern Cheyenne were taken prisoners. Their long-continued resistance was at last apparently convincing that these people of the north could not successfully be transplanted into the south. Their headquarters were, for a time following the capture of Little Wolf, at Fort Keogh, Montana, and in 1884 they were given a small, discouragingly sterile reservation on Tongue river, in Montana. Poverty and want have been largely the portion of these people on their reservation. Little can be expected through agriculture, as both opportunity and inclina-tion are lacking. Stock-raising, however, promises better days for this handful of people who so stubbornly held out for a tithe of what they rightly thought their own.

VI(1911), 92–94, 99–103

Disease and Drunkenness Attack the Piegan

It is difficult to present anything like a satisfactory estimate of the Piegan population previous to their observation by white men. [Alexander] Mackenzie, who saw them in 1789, was probably the first explorer to note their number. His estimate was from twenty-two hundred and fifty to twenty-five hundred and fifty warriors, or perhaps eighty-five hundred souls. [Alexander] Henry, the younger, in 1808 gave the population of the associated tribes as fourteen hundred and twenty warriors or six hundred and fifty tents. It is safe to estimate in this instance that there were eight to a tent, but if the extreme estimate of ten to a tent be allowed, it gives but sixty-five hundred. It is possible that Henry did not include all the bands. In the interest of trade it was the business of both Mackenzie and Henry to determine as accurately as possible the population of the different tribes with which they were to deal, hence it is safe to assume that their count was fairly accurate, Mackenzie's probably being nearer right.

Henry ... tells of their having suffered a serious attack of smallpox in 1781. Yet he does not speak of the epidemic as though it were an extraordinary one, as he no doubt would have done had it been similar to the scourge which almost annihilated

22 In the Piegan lodge of Little Plume and his son, Yellow Kidney, the tobacco pipe between them

the Mandan in 1837. Also, had they suffered from the disease to such a remarkable degree, Mackenzie would doubtless have mentioned it. It is not likely that the tribe lost in this first smallpox attack more than a third of its population. Granting such a loss, and assuming Mackenzie's figures to be approximately correct, we may regard the three tribes as having had an early population of practically twelve thousand. They suffered again from small-pox in 1838, and also in 1845. In 1855 Governor Stevens, while on his famous treaty expedition, estimated their population to be eighty-five hundred and thirty. Following this they once more suffered from smallpox in 1857, and again in 1869 the same disease swept over the prairies. In the winter of 1864 the three tribes lost about seventeen hundred and eighty by measles. The agent reported that the Bloods alone left standing in their plague-stricken camp five hundred death-lodges as silent monuments of the winter's devastation. The Indians were inclined to attribute this disease to the malevolence of the white men, suggesting that it was sent them in their annuity goods.

Hand in hand with pestilence stalked the liquor traffic, a foe scarcely less pernicious, and indeed they must have been a hardy and prolific people to have so well maintained their population against such maleficent odds. Disease was the white man's first bequest to them, and smallpox spread in advance of the traders and trappers. Quickly following, as a fit ally in the distribution of death, came the whiskey sellers, whose chief object was so to debauch the natives that their furs and other trafficable property could be secured as cheaply as possible. The usual procedure in the region was that when a party of Indians came to the trading post, they were first given sufficient liquor to intoxicate them, that they might be free in their traffic, and by the time they recovered from this debauch their furs were in possession of the traders. The argument of the traders was that they were to be commended for getting the Indians' furs for the least possible return, as the less whiskey the natives had the better off they were. Alexander Henry, the younger, who was a pioneer in this despicable traffic, and who was as lacking in illusions or in sentiment as any man who ever put his thoughts on paper, expatiated on the painful effects of the white man's invasion. Any conduct in association with the Indian, pernicious enough to arouse sympathy in the heart of Henry, must indeed have been incomprehensible to a man of the present civilization.

Fate, apparently not yet content with its dispensation to the Blackfeet tribes, dealt them another blow in the winter of 1883–1884, when more than one-fourth of the Piegan died of starvation —six hundred was the exact number recorded. There were, however, many other deaths in isolated camps, of which no record was made. This winter of misery and death was the result of official stupidity, coupled with the disappearance of the buffalo. Dr. George Bird Grinnell, in *Blackfoot Lodge Tales*, so graphically describes that fearful winter that further words would be useless.

A study of the Piegan conflict with white people, either citizens or soldiers, gives but a scant harvest, and shows that, considering their number and their provocation, they were one of the most harmless of tribes. It is true that in the popular press the name Blackfoot or Piegan was continually associated with massacre, outrage, and treachery. This, however, was but a habit without justification in fact. Such crime as they were guilty of was usually the direct result of drink, for which 'civilization' was wholly responsible, and such murders as they committed were simply the price we paid for the privilege of debauching them. Few tribes have been so unfortunate in this respect as the Blackfoot group. They dwelt partially in the United States and partially in Canada, and the traders and traffickers under each government vied with one another in wrecking them. Each side with whom they dealt in their international existence did all it could to incite the Indians to reprisal on the other government. The average Indian, who has but one people and one government with which to contend, is generally deserving of much sympathy, but when he is a victim of two governments and their subjects, he is unfortunate indeed.

Washo Contact with the White Man

The first white men in Washo territory were the trappers under Jedediah S. Smith, who passed through on their way to California in 1825. Explorers, trappers, and finally gold-seekers and colonists came in growing numbers. In 1846 the Donner party, bound for Sacramento valley, attempted to cross the mountains too late in the season and became snowbound at a small lake northwest of Tahoe. The father and the grandfather of the present Washo informant used to fish every year in Donner lake. One spring when they went there as usual, they were astonished to see a group of log huts. On the walls were guns and clothing. The use of these things they did not know. Outside were many corpses. Some of the bones seemed to have been sawed, and evidently cannibalism had been practised. They reported the discovery to their people, and with a larger party returned to the place. They saw where limbs thirty feet from the ground had been cut off for fuel during the winter, the deep snow having raised the prevailing level that distance.

The arrival of settlers was followed by the usual depredations and reprisals. The Washo however did not fall victims to organized warfare.

Although no general reservation has ever been assigned them, in 1892 they received allotments in severalty. A few were for-

23 Curtis considered these Washo baskets some of the most beautiful he had seen

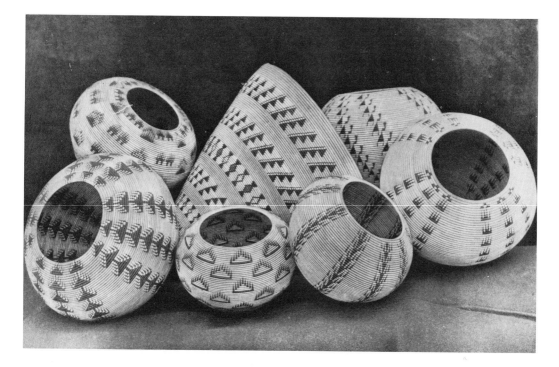

tunate enough to obtain tracts in the foothills where small areas can be cultivated, but many were assigned to barren slopes on the western side of Pine Nut range, a hopeless region which they have never occupied. The land is leased to sheep-raisers and returns a pitiful annual amount varying from a few cents to several dollars per family. The allotment of the Pine Nut lands is said to have resulted from a misunderstanding on the part of an interpreter. The spokesman for the Washo requested protection of the piñons, not allotment of the land.

In 1916 Congress appropriated ten thousand dollars for the purchase of land and water for the Washo, and five thousand dollars for their support and civilization. Five separate tracts aggregating 236 acres were purchased. The largest, consisting of 119 acres of sandy sagebrush land with little water, was occupied by three families in 1924. Twenty acres of rocky ground near Reno, costing six thousand dollars, was the home of a small number of Washo and Paviotso. On a tract of about forty acres five miles from Gardnerville a dozen families have erected cabins. But since a single well is the only source of water, successful tillage is out of the question. One man has sowed a plot of wheat about his house, desiring not only food for his family but fodder for his horses and a lawn to please the eye. He carries water in buckets from the well. Such ambition would seem to deserve better opportunities.

XV(1926), 90–91

U.S. Government treatment of the Indians of California

While it is not the purpose of [my work] to dwell largely on the wrongs of the Indians, in the present instance it is impossible to evade this distressing subject entirely. All Indians suffered through the selfishness of our own race, but the natives of California were the greatest sufferers of all. They were not warlike. They consisted of small, isolated groups lacking the social instinct and the strength for self-defense against a force so strong as ours. By what was supposed to have been a treaty they signed away their lands, in lieu of which they were to be granted definite areas much smaller in extent, together with certain goods and chattels, and educational advantages. This treaty was never ratified, yet we took advantage of one of its proposed provisions by assuming immediate possession of the Indian lands, by which cunning the majority of the natives were left homeless. Little by little, tardily and grudgingly, action toward providing homes for the surviving unfortunates has been taken; but what has been granted them in most cases only intensifies the outrage, for many of the reservations are barren, rocky hillsides of less than an acre for each individual—land the tillage of which is next to impossible. The conditions are still so acute that, after spending many months among these scattered groups of Indians, the author finds it difficult even to mention the subject with calmness.

XIII(1924), xi–xii

24 A Hopi at Middle Mesa, Arizona, counting the record of losses inflicted on past invaders

25 *A Modern Yurok House* in the vicinity of the Klamath and Trinity Rivers, on the coast of Northern California

4 Religious Beliefs and Practices

Religious Beliefs of the Wichita

The pantheon of the Wichita compared with that of most tribes is rich in its inclusions, a richness which indicates more than the ordinary consideration of the Infinite. Such comprehension of the spirits and such definite theological conclusions as exist with these people may be looked for only among sedentary or semi-sedentary groups.

Kinnikasus is the foremost of supernatural beings. The Wichita definition of Kinnikasus is 'Man Never Known On Earth.' To amplify, it might be said 'Not Known To Man,' or beyond human knowledge. That which is beyond the understanding of man is necessarily the Infinite, hence Kinnikasus is the figure-head of the Infinite.

Kinnikasus was the creator; he created man and all things on the earth. In prayer the Wichita invoke many supernatural beings, but the invocation invariably includes Kinnikasus as the Spirit Over All.

In personification and deification of the animate and inanimate, a definite division of the divine ones is made—the sky gods and the earth gods. So pronounced is the consideration of the stars and planets that a hasty conclusion might class their beliefs as astrolatry, yet it is most unlikely that the religion of any people ever could have been correctly so regarded. Each myth character bears a name, which analyzed describes the function of the personage; for example, . . . 'Bright Shining Woman', the moon, and . . . 'Woman Forever In The Water', the spirit of the water.

As previously stated, Man Never Known On Earth is the fore-most figure of the pantheon. The Morning Star, Having Power To Carry Light, is the spirit of the first man created. He was the prophet teacher of the people and is included in most prayers.

The next character is of utmost importance in Wichita mythology. It is the spirit of the moon, Bright Shining Woman. The moon was the first woman created, and the wife of Morning Star, thus was the mother of the universe. This goddess controls all things feminine or procreative. It matters not whether it is human birth, the propagation of animals, or the planting of crops—all come within the province of the Moon Goddess. On

approaching motherhood a woman constantly implores her beneficence, and the new-born child is held in outstretched hands to the moon while the mother prays that it may grow strong and have long life.

The sun is Man Reflecting Light. His advent followed Morning Star and Moon; in fact, his creation was the first important act of Morning Star. The Wichita insist that the sun is an important spirit, yet their concepts do not bear out that claim. Rarely is the spirit of the sun included in their invocations. Indirect information suggests that there is an unexpressed, indefinable association between Man Never Known On Earth and Spirit Of The Sun, almost to the extent that the two are one and the same. The obvious anachronism is not greater than is often found in mythology and theology.

The spirit of the water, Woman Forever In The Water, is closely associated with the Moon Spirit, yet their functions differ: one creates life, the other makes possible its growth, its continuation. As an illustration, a woman desiring a child would not pray to the Water Spirit, but would address her supplication to the Spirit Of The Moon; then when the child was born the mother implored the beneficence of the Water Spirit, the Moon Spirit, and included the supreme spirit, Man Not Known On Earth.

A special function of the Water Spirit is to guard the virtue of women. During their husbands' absence on the warpath or the hunt, wives went each day to the river to bathe, and to pray to the Water Spirit, begging that she protect them from disaster. They would include the Morning Star and the Moon Spirit in their prayers. Even in the changed conditions today, this theory and practice remain.

The earth is Earth Mother, the mother of all life. From her man was created and upon his death he returns to her bosom. From her body sprang all things which nourished and maintained man. Wind is life, the breath of the Earth Mother, and is associated with the soul. Wind as here referred to is not associated with the four cardinal points.

The South Star is special guardian of the male; its beneficence gives the man vigorous sons and guards him in warfare.

The North Star, The Light Which Stands Still, is to be feared; it brings death, yet it also gives life. Perhaps it gives life through withholding death. The medicine-men look to this spirit to assist them in their healing rites. In all probability the healers in imploring this spirit are in fact begging him to stay his icy hand.

In the west is 'The Light That Flies,' that is, meteors. This spirit of the west has also power to aid in healing sickness. An unidentified faint star at the zenith, personified as 'Flint Stone Lying Down Above,' is included as a spirit in many invocations.

As indicated in the culture legends, animals often become

beneficent spirits. Such spirits should not be confused with the Sky spirits or gods, but rather should be viewed as personal-property spirits, in that the recipient for a consideration could transfer power or knowledge so received.

As with the majority of American Indians, the concept of after-life is vague. Immortality, through belief in or desire for it, is accepted. The belief that the afterworld or spirit land is some-where in the sky seemingly antedates any contact with missionary teaching. The celestial location of their spirit land is the obvious conclusion of a people whose religious beliefs centralize so completely around the stars and planets.

The state of existence in the afterworld is a natural creation born of human desire, a life of happiness free from all earthly discomfort. Seemingly the only insurmountable bar to entrance into this heaven is suicide. The spirits of those who commit self-murder may hover near and be conscious of the delights of heaven, but may not enter.

XIX(1930), 44–46

Child Fetishes of the Santo Domingo Keres

For every girl a wooden doll . . . is made by one of her male relatives. The material is either cottonwood or Douglas spruce, and the doll, about twelve inches long, may be either cylindrical or flat. Having rudely carved a face, the man goes to the head of any shaman society and asks that his doll be painted and decorated in the manner of some certain kind of Shiwanna, if a male baby is desired for the girl, or in the manner of Kochi-nako ('yellow maid'), a mythic character, if a female child is desired.

The bringing of such a fetish to the girl for whom it is desig-nated is an incident of a Shiwanna dance. A single file of masked figures approaches the pueblo, led by Heruta and the man who carries the doll, who is regarded as its father. The Kusari clowns as usual interpret for Heruta. After entering the village the Shiwanna crowd about the 'father' of the doll, caressing it, calling it by endearing terms, and urging it to remain in this pueblo with a good heart, promising to come frequently to see if it is treated well and to bring it gifts. The 'father' gives the fetish to the girl for whom it is intended, whose relatives crowd about her, each holding out a pinch of meal, upon which she breathes and which they then offer to the Shiwanna. The fruits and corn brought by the gods are piled up on two or three baskets, in which they are borne by the Kusari to the girl's house. Imme-diately her relatives lead her home, and a few women hasten ahead to prepare a bed for the childbirth. If the girl is very young, her mother now takes her place. The girl (or her mother) at once goes to bed, and the women proceed to boil a large quantity of water with crushed juniper-leaves and -berries.

In childbirth Santo Domingo women take a position on hands and knees, with a pad under the abdomen. In this position the

27 A Piegan medicine man with his sacred pipe

child is expelled. A Flint shaman stands beside the woman, advising her how to exert her strength whenever the labor pains occur. If the infant cannot be expelled, he gives manual assistance. In any case he does what he can by pressing on the abdomen. The umbilical cord is cut with a flint knife, the placenta is wrapped in an old blanket and thrown into the Rio Grande. The navel-cord, when it sloughs off, is buried beneath the floor. After delivering her child, the mother is heavily wrapped about the loins with blankets and other cloths, and all openings in the house are closed, to induce perspiration. She drinks a large quantity of warm water containing crushed juniper-berries and -leaves. Parents hoping for a male child hang a bow and an arrow outside the house, and for a female child a besom, a bundle of sticks used in stirring parching corn, and a parching-vessel.

The girl having taken the position assumed by a woman in parturition, the wooden doll is placed under her body, and after a period of groaning and physical exertion, which results in profuse sweating, the shaman inserts his hand under her, draws out the doll, and shows a small quantity of blood. He lays the doll in the bed with its 'mother,' and it is attended just as if it were an infant of flesh and blood. On the fourth day it is taken out 'to let the sun see it,' and it receives a name, and it is then laid in a small swinging cradle suspended from a roof-beam. Every day it is 'fed' with meal. Some informants say they have seen women nursing their dolls, others deny that this is done. A certain woman, mother of four adult children, recently received a doll from the Shiwanna at the age of about sixty years.

The dolls are attended daily, and when the 'mother' dies her dolls are given to some younger female of the house, who thenceforth takes care of them. They are never buried or otherwise disposed of, and they are a permanent fixture in the household. Some houses have as many as fifteen.

XVI(1926), 161–162

The Potency of Charm Words for Coastal Salish Peoples

Among all these Salish tribes there existed a belief in the potency of charm words, which were handed down from parent to child through many generations. The power inherent is such words was known in the Nisqualli dialect as *swiduq*. Generally the words were fanciful, having significance only to those who used them. In the heat of battle a fighter might suddenly halt, slap his thighs, arms, chest, and head, call them by secret names, and thus become imbued with renewed strength and courage. When a storm threatened to swamp a canoe, the occupant might slap its gunwales and address it by some charm name, which would give it power to resist the storm and come to land. But the chief use of these expressions was in acquiring and holding the love of another. If a young man wished to win the attention

28 The facade of San Xavier del Bac, the church built by early Spanish missionaries at the centre of Papago lands in Southern Arizona

of a girl, he would call her heart by some secret name, repeating the word whenever he saw her, and this, it was thought, would cause her soon to fall in love with him. Women especially were given to this practice. If a woman were deserted by a husband whom she greatly loved, she would name his heart and his feet, repeating the phrases over and over, trying thus to cause his heart to yearn for her and his feet to bring him back. When her charm succeeded, it became in demand by others and was sold at a high price. Canoes, slaves, and goods aggregating hundreds of dollars in value were gladly exchanged for a charm that had proved itself potent. A formula used by Wahelchu, a Suquamish, for preservation in a storm is addressed to the sun: ... 'Take care of me, O Bright-faced One, the Sun! Take care of me, Water on which I rest, and you, Dry Land!' IX(1913), 111–112

Nez Percé Fasting

[The Nez Percé] must have dwelt in a veritable wonderland. As a man passed through the forest the moving trees whispered to him and his heart swelled with the song of the swaying pine. He looked through the green branches and saw white clouds drifting across the blue dome, and he felt the song of the clouds. Each bird twittering in the branches, each water-fowl among the reeds or on the surface of the lake, spoke its intelligible message to his heart; and as he looked into the sky and saw the high-flying birds of passage, he knew that their flight was made strong by the uplifted voices of ten thousand birds of the meadow, forest, and lake, and his heart, fairly in tune with all this, vibrated with the songs of its fulness. Indians with a simple system in which the individual possessed only the spirit of the bird or the beast revealed to him are indeed close to nature, but the individual Nez Percé, with his interwoven devotional system, communed with almost unlimited nature.

The Nez Percé began his preparation for spiritual attainment almost in infancy. The child, either boy or girl, when less than ten years of age was told by the father or the mother that it was time to have *tiwatitmas*—spiritual power. 'This afternoon you must go to yonder mountain and fast. When you reach the place of fasting, build a fire and do not let it die. As the Sun goes down, sit on the rocks facing him, watch while he goes from sight, and look in that direction all night. When the dawn comes, go to the east and watch the Sun return to his people. When he comes to noon, go to the south and sit there, and when he has travelled low again, go to the west where you sat first and watch until he is gone. Then start for your home.' After some sacred object, such as a feather, had been tied to the child's clothing, and a few parting words of instruction and encouragement had been given, the little suppliant was sent on its journey.

What a picture of Indian character this affords: a mere infant starting out alone into the fastnesses of the mountain wilds, to commune with the spirits of the infinite, a tiny child sitting through the night on a lonely mountain-top, reaching out its infant's hands to God! On distant and near-by hills howl the coyote and the wolf. In the valleys and on the mountain side prowl and stalk all manner of animals. Yet alone by the little fire sits the child listening to the mysterious voices of the night.

For its first fasting a child was sent as far as from Lapwai to Lake Waha, or to Taiya-mahsh, a mountain twelve miles to the south. The child was familiar with the country and knew the trails because the father had often talked to it and told it of the nature of the land, pointing out the direction and saying that yonder was a place of fasting. There was no ceremony of purification before setting out, as the child was assumed to be pure. On ridges in the mountains were places already prepared for the fasters, the makers now unknown, as the monuments have been there time out of memory. They consist of piles of stones about two feet high, arcs of circles, one with the opening to the east, another open to the west, a third to the south. Within these sat the faster, changing from one to the other as the sun moved from east to west, and passing the night sleeplessly in the western arc. He neither ate nor drank during the period of fasting, which sometimes lasted two nights and a day.

As the time approached when the faster was expected to return, the mother prepared a feast, and when the food was given to him it was first blown upon by a medicine-man in order to purify it and make it beneficial to the faster. All the family and the visitors ate with him. He was not asked and did not tell of his vigil. Perhaps the child a short time later was sent out again, either to the same place or to a new one. Thus before reaching the age of fifteen he might have been fasting in the mountains from five to ten times. In these fastings, boys sometimes remained out three nights and two days, and in rare cases twice that number. A youth having passed the period of continence never fasted, for, if he had, he would have experienced no visions, being impure.

Vision creatures appearing in vigils did not always confer a name on the faster. When they did, it referred to the creature

29 The Kwakiutl believed that during an eclipse the sun had swallowed the moon, so they burned old, smelly and distasteful things ceremonially to make him sneeze and disgorge the moon

itself, and was assumed by the faster only after he had been to war. Thereafter he was known by that name. Thus a man's medicine cannot always be discerned from his name. A boy might, after returning from his vigil, say to his father, 'I have seen something, and I have a name,' but he would not tell what he had seen or what the name was. After singing his song for the first time in the long-house medicine ceremony, he would reveal his name to his father and ask that the people be told. Then the father would make a feast and announce the son's name.

A description of an actual vision is very difficult to obtain from the Nez Percés. Three Eagles, however, thus describes what one might see if thunder appeared to him in his vigil: 'The faster sees a man coming, and goes to him. He appears to be a man wrapped in a yellow blanket, and he gives the boy whatever he may be carrying. The little boy, if he could be seen now, would be found lying as if dead. When he awakens he may think, "I met a man." That is all he would remember.'

Here are shown two very interesting points: that the boy when receiving his revelation or vision is 'lying as if dead,' and that when he awakens there seems but a vague recollection of what occurred. Both of these statements indicate that the visions are not usually had while in a natural sleep, but while in hypnosis. In fact, the Indians continually repeat that it is not in a normal sleep that visions are experienced, but ever state that 'I lay as if dead.'

If, in these pilgrimages, the youth did not receive visions, he would then have to resort to sweating, fasting, and purification. In such cases, at about the age of twenty years, he went in the company of an assistant to some stream and there dug a hole large enough to admit his body, and filled it with water. Then, after heating to redness a large number of stones, the suppliant disrobed, took three or four red-osier wands the thickness of a lead-pencil and the length of his body from throat to waist, and thrust them, one by one, far down his throat. Each stick was left in the throat until the red bark just outside the mouth turned gray (probably with spittle), and the removal of each caused vomiting. It was imagined that 'different colors of fever' could be seen in the discharge. Then he took from a large bundle of wands an equal number (three or four), and thrust them also down his throat. If during these first two operations the supposedly foul matter which was believed to be defiling his body came out in the form of 'differently colored fevers,' he might cease this part of the purification, or he might repeat it as many times as he wished, but each time he used the same number of sticks as he started with, either three or four. If the impurities were not discharged the first or the second time, then he used the three or four sticks fifteen times. Next he went into the pit and sat down, the water coming up to his shoulders, and he dropped the heated stones in, making it as hot as he could bear. When darkness fell, he emerged, went to his lodge, and slept in a sitting posture, so that the matter which was believed to be in his system would pass downward. It would have been dangerous to sleep lying on the back, because the impurities would have formed more matter in the bones and chest. In the morning the suppliant went to the same place, heated the stones, took wands from the bundle, and thrust them down his throat, which now was so swollen that the sticks were inserted with some difficulty, and as it continued to swell he was obliged to assist the entrance by the muscular action of swallowing. When he could do no more he threw the stones into the water, sat down in it, and bathed there all day without eating or drinking. At sunset he returned to his lodge and slept again, sitting. Again on the third day he heated the stones and bathed all day long, coming out only to heat more stones, but he did not thrust any of the wands down his throat. Thus he continued for seven days in all (in addition to the first two days when wands were used), spending each night in a sitting posture in his lodge. After returning on the last day he was given a very soft kind of soup, for in addition to the weakened condition of his stomach, his throat was too raw to permit the passage of solid food.

When the faster had recovered, he was able to run without fatigue up steep hills. To him the 'deer was like a dead animal,' that is, it could not scent the man because all the earthly odor had been removed from him. The man who had thus purified himself was a far better hunter than one who had not, even though the latter had 'hunting medicine' obtained in vision. In some cases this purification was followed by baths in ice-water. When the first ice formed, the man went to the edge of the stream about nine in the morning, broke the ice and stood in the water up to his neck, remaining as long as he could, then emerged and sat on the bank without covering. Then again he went into the water, and out again, and back for a third bath. Thus the time from mid-morning until noon was broken into periods for three or four baths and three or four exposures to sun and air, or if the man was especially hardy, into two such periods. This was done each day until spring. Both this practice and that of the vomiting and hot baths are carried on to-day.

VIII(1911), 62–66

The Inter-Tribal Peyote Cult

The Peyote cult as it exists today can be considered in many ways as the most interesting religious organization among the North American Indians. The cult is predicated upon the use of peyote—a variety of cactus growing in Texas and northern Mexico. An important feature of the ceremony is the eating of the peyote 'button,' the small core at the centre of the plant. The members of the society are referred to sometimes as Peyote-eaters.

At a meeting of the fraternity, the members eat from four to two or three dozen of these buttons. The effect of the peyote is stimulating, perhaps more to the brain than the body, and in no way resembles alcoholic stimulation. The use of this cactus bulb by the priesthoods among the Indians of northern Mexico and the southwestern states is no doubt of considerable antiquity. It was a part of their ceremonial paraphernalia. In gathering ethnologic data from Indians of the Southwest, many fragments of information have been revealed to indicate the use of peyote by medicine-men as a stimulant.

As an organized cult, Peyote in the United States is of introduction later than the first contact with the white race. According to the best information obtainable, the White Mountain Apache of Arizona were the first to establish the Peyote ceremony. The next tribe to acquire it was the Jicarilla Apache of northern New Mexico. From them it was adopted by the Comanche.

From the Comanche the Peyote cult spread rapidly through many of the tribes of the Southwest, beginning about the year 1886. Now it is the most highly organized religious movement among tribes of that region, and it extends northward to the Indians of Idaho, Montana, and the Dakotas. Wherever the Peyote cult has been introduced, the majority of tribesmen are adherents of its teachings. It is claimed by Peyote leaders that in

30 Altar Peyote with Rattles— Osage

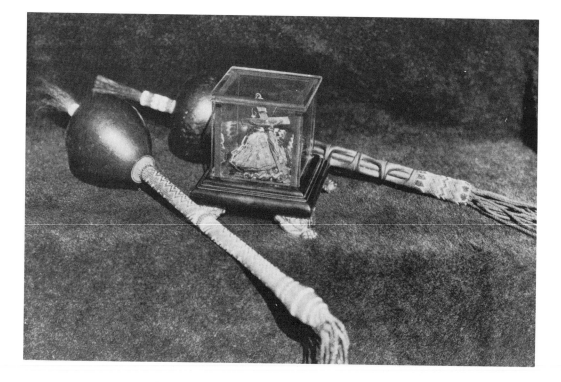

Oklahoma, aside from members of the Five Civilized Tribes, all Indians of stability are members, while those who have not come under its influence are of the dissolute class. Occasionally, however, one finds an individual whose Christian beliefs are so firmly established that he refuses to join the order.

The formula of the ritual, if it may be so termed, is a blending of Christianity and Indian ceremony which varies in minor details according to the religious bent of the particular leader. Among Peyote leaders may be found devout Catholics, Mormons, Mennonites, Baptists, and Methodists. In fact, among its members are representatives of every Christian denomination in the tribe in which the cult is practised; indeed the majority of its members are adherents also of some Christian church.

Among the Southern Cheyenne, one of the foremost exponents of the Peyote cult, and a full-blood, is an ordained minister. He has been a member of the cult for forty years, joining shortly after the organization took root among his people and while the membership was small. So far as can be learned, the cult is not antagonistic to Christianity. There may, however, at times be opposition to individual missionaries who are overzealous in their antagonism to it.

The Mormon church seemingly is not opposed, and the Catholic church makes little protest. All other Christian organizations, however, are unanimous in their opposition, notwithstanding the fact that the teachings of Peyotism are designed to promote moral living and sobriety, and its foremost tenet is to do good to one's fellow men.

Indian religion, that is, instinctive worship of the divine ones, or the Infinite, does not of itself necessarily embody a moral code, and in this respect the Peyote formula differs from other Indian cults. No dancing or levity forms a part of the Peyote meeting; rather, it is a night of song, prayer, and meditation, preceded in most cases by a sweat-bath in order that the body may be freed from earthly contamination.

So far as can be learned, the formula of songs is the same wherever the Peyote order exists. Notwithstanding the fact that the Indians claim that the White Mountain Apache of Arizona were the first to establish the ceremony as it exists in the United States today, the ritual is obviously copied from Wichita ceremonial form. Most of the words of the songs and prayers are Comanche. The type of drum used is always the same—a small iron kettle partly filled with water and having a rawhide head. The beating of the drum is continuous throughout the rite, and its rhythmic vibration undoubtedly affects the emotions of the participants. A well-informed leader stated that the exhilaration of the worshippers is the combined effect of the drumbeat and the peyote. The order of the prayers is the same, but their wording varies according to the fluency and sect of the leader.

At all meetings a fine selected specimen of peyote is placed upon the crescent altar, and if the leader should be a Catholic, there rests across the peyote a crucifix. Prayers include the divine ones of the Indians, as well as God and the Son of God. The code of the cult demands upright living to an extent that should be satisfactory to any church, and it takes a positive stand against the use of intoxicants. In fact, the Peyote men claim that they have no desire for liquor, even though they may once have been drunkards.

An important feature of Peyotism is the healing of disease. Many remarkable cures are cited, but to what extent they may be credited to the medicinal properties of peyote is an open question. The cures are so many and so well authenticated that even the skeptic must accept the facts; and unless the plant possesses unique curative properties, Peyotism is far in advance of other mental-healing cults. To snatch countless people from the graves of consumptives is no mean achievement, even if it requires a combination of medicine and mental healing. The teaching of the cult is not to regard peyote as a medicine in the literal sense, but rather that through the use of this one of 'God's plants' the believer may receive aid from divine sources.

Notwithstanding this dogma, it is the opinion of the writer that the Peyote-cult teachers depend more on the literal than the spiritual. The strength of this hybrid cult no doubt may be attributed to the belief that it is something that comes from within, God-given to the Red Race. Its ritualistic form is the Indians' own, slightly colored by Christian contact. A Caucasian spectator at one of these meetings could well imagine himself to be listening to the incantations of primitive priests, unless by chance he should catch the words 'Jesus Christ, the Son of God,' from a chant.

The cult has not gained its present foothold without opposition from medicine-men and the priesthood of the tribes among which it thrives. In fact, in many of the pueblos of Arizona and New Mexico the opposition of the Indian priests has been strong enough to prevent it from becoming established except at Taos.

The symbol of the organization is the crescent, and the writer well remembers the early years of the order of the crescent on the White Mountain Apache reservation. Peyote at that time was not mentioned in connection with the society, and the fight against the crescent group was a bitter one. The old-time Apache medicine-men were a power among their people, and, jealous of their position, they united in a bitter fight against the new cult, which at that time was shrouded by the greatest possible secrecy. The medicine-man who led the new order claimed that he had received the songs in a vision. Among these people, as elsewhere, Peyotism has swept all before it, and it is doubtful if there is now a medicine-man among the Apache of Arizona who is not a member of the order.

The Peyote organization is the only one in which the most devout adherent of Christianity and the most conservative medicine-men work side by side. Opposition by the white race to the use of peyote has dragged through all the years of its existence. Worshippers have been arrested, indicted, and tried in state courts. Failing of conviction there, they have been taken before the Federal courts, again without conviction. In Oklahoma an attempt was made to enact a law to make the use of peyote a crime, but in that state the situation has been somewhat cleared by the securing of a charter for the cult, under which the organization is legally called the 'Native American Church.'

A partially effective blow to the use of peyote is a ruling against its interstate shipment; but this does not prevent an Indian of any state from driving to Texas and returning with a supply if he so desires. Opposition has so stimulated the Peyote cult movement that its membership is steadily increasing. The limit of its diffusion is seemingly racial only.

To appreciate the hold that Peyotism now has on the Indian, one needs an intimate knowledge of his metamorphic religious state—a more comprehensive term would be his muddled religious state. It must be borne in mind that the greater number of the cult members are under the influence of Christian teachings, but with only a vague idea of what is in the minds of their teachers. Yet many of the Indians who are so far advanced that they are preachers in the respective church organizations of which they are members, still cling to the primitive beliefs of their fathers without a qualm. [To quote one man:]

When I listened to the white teacher, he told us of a new God; said there was but one God and that he was in his church and not anywhere else. Then my heart was sad. For a long time I thought about the white man's God. Then my heart told me that is was not a new God all in one church, but, as our fathers taught us, the Universal Spirit was everywhere, and that what the preacher was telling us of his God was only the all-present Spirit which we knew so well. When I tried to tell the preacher that my heart was glad, that I now understood his God was the same as ours, then my friend the missionary became angry and told me not to think of the Spirit Over All but to pray to God.

[Typical experiences of Peyote people follow, and with alcoholism a problem among Indians, it is encouraging to report that numerous members of the order say they have lost all desire to drink. (Also, it should be remembered that the peyote,— while a powerful drug and though consumed in large quantities during the night-long ceremonies—is handled reverentially not indiscriminately, ritualistically not casually in the way that alcohol is used.)]

A Cheyenne, forty-eight years of age, educated at Carlisle, worked in the hospital there. After leaving school he was employed in other Indian hospitals. Becoming a confirmed drunkard, according to his own statements, his chief object in life was to obtain whiskey; he would do anything for a drink. He so neglected his wife and children that others had to clothe and feed them, until his wife was finally compelled to leave him. He had no interest in his tribesmen; even should they be in distress, he was quite indifferent to their suffering. Once a man of fine physique, he became so emaciated that he weighed only one hundred and forty-five pounds. Once after a drinking debauch he was run over by a wagon and his chest crushed.

While still an invalid, friends persuaded him to join the Peyote organization. After becoming a member, he not only drank no intoxicants, but claims that the craving completely left him and that at no time does he desire to drink. Within a few years he has become one of the most substantial men of the tribe, living in a good home, with his children well cared for. He cultivates his own farm and proudly boasts that no member of his tribe can grow more wheat to the acre than he; and with greater pride asserts that if any member of his tribe is in trouble or distress, 'I shall always do everything I can to help him, and that makes me happy.'

A Ponca man of sixty years relates: 'I was just like a skeleton; I had tuberculosis; I was almost dead, and weighed but ninety-five pounds. I went to see some white doctors. They looked at me and said: "You are the same as dead; you should go home and die. Do not spend money to talk with doctors; save your money to buy a coffin."

'Then my friend said, "You had better join the Peyote; perhaps that will make you well." I became a member of the Peyote society and took peyote all the time. Soon I grew stronger. In three months I was almost a strong man. In a year I was like a young man and had nearly doubled my weight. Before I joined the Peyote I did not care how other people lived. They might be hungry, but that did not concern me. Now I always think about other people, and all the Indians know that if they are hungry they can come to me.'

XIX(1930), 199–203, 213

76

5 Tribal Organisation

Apache Tribal Organization

The clan and gentile systems of the American Indians have been the bulwark of their social structure, for by preventing inter-marriage within the clan or the gens the blood was kept at its best. Added to this were the hardships of the Indian life, which resulted in the survival only of the fittest and provided the foundation for a sturdy people. But with advancing civilization one forsees the inevitable disintegration of their tribal laws, and a consequent weakening of the entire social structure. [The Apache nation is made up of a number of large sub-groups such as the Coyoteros and the Chiricahua, and these in turn consist of smaller groups.]

The Coyoteros are divided into five bands, each consisting of a number of clans, although in one band there are now survivors of a single clan only, while in others as many as seven or eight clans are still to be found. Descent among the Apache generally is reckoned through the mother; that is, the children belong to their mother's clan. An exception to this rule is said by 'Peaches', an old Apache scout under Crook, to exist among the Chiricahua, where the children take the gens of the father. Among the Apache some of the younger generation are inclined to disregard tribal laws respecting marriage, but in former times they were rigidly enforced, marriage within the clan or the gens being regarded as incestuous. When asked what would happen if a man and a woman belonging to the same clan should marry, one old man answered that both would be quickly put to death. ... Geronimo, Chato, and Cochise were members of the ... People of the East clan. Most of the clan names are derived from localities in which the ancestors of the clan are supposed to have first lived.

With the Apache, as with other tribes, the clan organization has an important bearing on property right. Regardless of what property either spouse may hold or own at the time of marriage, the other immediately becomes possessed of his or her moiety. Should the wife die, her husband retains possession of the property held in common so long as he does not remarry, but what might be termed the legal ownership of the wife's half interest becomes

77

vested in her clan. Should he attempt to dissipate the property the members of the deceased wife's clan would at once interfere. If the widower wishes to marry again and the woman of his choice belongs to the clan of his former wife, then he and the new wife become owners in common of all personal property held by him; but if the second wife belongs to a different clan from that of the former wife, then the husband must make actual transfer of half of the common property to the clanspeople of the deceased woman, who inherited the legal interest in it at their relative's death. The same tribal law applies in the case of a widow.

Much internal strife naturally results whenever an actual distribution of property is made. In the first place the surviving spouse unwillingly relinquishes the moiety of the property to the relatives of the deceased, and the immediate relatives often

78

disagree with the remainder of the clan. In former times death of one or more members of contending clans often resulted when the division of much property was made. Having no tribunal for making an equitable division, the matter was left to mutual agreement, resulting in disputes and frequently murder.

With the breaking up of the clans, together with the rapid disintegration of ancient customs and laws, this property law is fast becoming forgotten; but so recently as 1906 such disputes as those mentioned occurred under both the Fort Apache and San Carlos agencies, creating no little ill-feeling. In one instance a man refused to deliver possession of half of his little herd of horses to his deceased wife's clanspeople when contemplating marriage with another woman, and appealed to the missionaries for aid. He was compelled to make the division, however, before he could remarry.

I(1907), 21–23

Teton Sioux (or Lakota) Tribal Government

Chiefs were elected at a general council of the men, led by the Short Hair Lodge and similar organizations. . . . The council was consulted on questions of public moment, such as laws governing the camp and, particularly, affecting the hunt. Small war-parties were made up without regard to the chiefs or the council, for any individual who could gain a following was free to go against the enemy. General rules were often suggested to the chiefs by the different societies.

Some of the young men, perhaps half of them, were organized into the Soldier Band. When the chiefs met, the Soldiers gathered at the council-place and took their position in front of the tipi, first having gone about the village gathering food for the councillors. If a man was asked to give a dog for the feast and refused, the Soldiers would kill the dog and take it away, and if resentment was shown they would punish the offender by destroying some of his property or by beating him. The Soldiers, in a way, were the servants of the chiefs, and consequently were supposed to carry out their instructions. If the chiefs decided to move camp on the following day, the Soldiers were so informed, and when morning came they mounted their horses, rode about the camp and made everybody pull down his tipi, and saw that all promptly took the trail. If one should refuse to obey the command, the Soldiers cut his tipi to pieces and killed a horse or two, and if the man gave vent to anger his life might be forfeited. Orders to move camp sometimes originated in the Soldier Lodge, but their action was only in the form of a suggestion to the chiefs, who agreed or not as they deemed fit.

The Soldiers of each village had two leaders, Soldier Chiefs, through whom all commands of the tribal chiefs were communicated to the lodge. When young men were sent out to look for buffalo, Soldiers kept guard so that only those authorized to

go could leave the village; and on the return of the scouts with report of where the buffalo were, they assumed charge of the preparations for the hunt, and saw that all started together. Some of the Soldiers remained at home, guarding the village, while others accompanied the huntsmen and kept them together until they had neared the herd. Any man who began to shoot before the signal was given was severely beaten, sometimes to insensibility, his horse probably killed, his clothing cut to pieces, and his gun or bow and arrows broken. If he showed the slightest resentment, he was quite likely to be killed. The same treatment was accorded one who should steal away from the party on the march and kill a lone buffalo even without alarming the herd. At times in the autumn several bands formed a single buffalo hunting party; on such occasions the Soldiers kept the entire party together, not permitting one band to leave the others until the hunting-grounds were reached, after which the scouts were sent out. When the buffalo were found, the band hunted together until every one had been supplied with enough meat for the winter. After the general hunt the chiefs gave the command to disband in order that the horses might have sufficient forage, as well as to avoid the sickness which experience taught them followed the practice of camping together in large numbers. This dispersion brought a partial disintegration of the Soldier Band, since each member accompanied his own patriarchal group.

The Soldiers had their headquarters in the large *tiyo-tipi*, pitched near the tipi of the head-chief, and it became a general rendezvous and lounging place for the members. If there was dearth of food in the lodge, a member was sent out to distribute through the camp a hundred red sticks, each a sign, not to be disregarded, that the recipient must quickly furnish meat to the *tiyo-tipi*. If a member of the body should keep the others waiting after a meeting had been called, he was treated rather roughly on his arrival; the injuries inflicted were not serious, consisting principally in the cutting up of his robe and other clothing.

Soldiers were appointed by the Soldier Chiefs, who donned their war-bonnets and rode from tipi to tipi, shaking the hand of each man chosen. To be selected a Soldier was a distinct honor, to which only men of tried courage and strength, who had counted at least one undisputed coup, could aspire. Red Cloud, before he became a chief, was always chosen Soldier Chief, for, being a man of indomitable courage, he carried out the chief's orders with reckless disregard of consequences.

In addition to the Soldier Lodge there were several other societies, or lodges, one of the most important being that of the Brave Hearts. . . . All plains tribes had similar orders, the function of which in all cases was practically the same. The paraphernalia of the organization among the Ogalala were two buffalo head-

32 *Chief Garfield.* When the Jicarilla were officially made to adopt Spanish or English names this head-chief chose the name of former President James Garfield

81

dresses, four lances, a drum, and two quirts, and its purpose was to inspire its members to acts of bravery and the succor of those in danger or in need. From the membership of the society were selected four men with brave hearts to carry the lances, and two others to act as attendants in the lodge. It was occasionally necessary to obtain recruits. In selecting them, members would go to the tipis and lead forth the young men who were thought worthy. Sometimes a man would object to becoming a member and even after being taken to the society's tipi might make his escape. Such action was regarded as a great and lasting disgrace. If, on the other hand, the candidate remained, he was lauded by the people, for he thus avowed himself ready at any time to give up his life to the enemy. The men who bore the lances in battle were exposed to the gravest danger, however, since when their comrades were hard pressed, one of them was in duty bound to plant his staff in the ground and remain by it until all of his party had passed that point. He was then called *Igulashka*, He Ties Himself, and, like the color-bearer, was not supposed to retreat.

On the death of a lance-bearer a member was chosen to take his place. Owing to the great danger involved, the position was necessarily regarded as one of high honor, and to refuse it when proffered would subject a warrior to ineffaceable disgrace. An expression of the utmost derision was, 'He would not take the lance!'

Another society was the Short Hair. ... This is a modern designation, used only within the last fifty years, the old name being ... Wear Buffalo Head-dresses. The short buffalo-hair of the head-dresses gave rise to the modern name. Only warriors of renown were eligible, men who had gained undisputed honors, and they were appointed, rather than elected, by the four chiefs of the tribe. When a warrior was deemed worthy of membership, the Soldier Chiefs were sent for, and he was brought to the tipi, placed before the chiefs, and told of the honor conferred

34 This Oto chief, Old Eagle, wears a peace medal of the type distributed by most presidents to Indian leaders who journeyed to Washington

on him. An address of advice was made to him, and his relatives distributed such gifts as were expected of those to whom distinction had come. The members of this society are said to have had the elective power of new chiefs.

The Teton Sioux had several other societies whose functions were much the same—that of encouraging the members to deeds of bravery and to perform acts of hospitality and liberality. Rivalry always existed between the different organizations as to which had the most aggressive and fearless leaders and the bravest men.

III(1908), 12–16

The Kwakiutl Economic System

At the base of the whole [Kwakiutl] social system lies the potlatch, or distribution of property among the assembled people. Together with the practice of lending at interest, it provides for a communistic life. No individual can starve or be in serious want so long as there is any property in the possession of the tribe; for there are frequent distributions of goods, and if the individual becomes needy in the meantime, he can always borrow at interest. If, when the principal and interest fall due, fortune still refuses to smile on him, he simply borrows another amount sufficient to pay. Thus debts may accumulate until payment is hopeless, a condition said to be particularly frequent in the case of women. On the other hand many a woman is the business manager of the family, and a very canny one too, able to repeat without an error and without ocular aids to memory the names of her scores of debtors and creditors and the respective amounts of the miscellaneous accounts, which include everything from pots to canoes.

The potlatch is intimately bound up with the life of the family. Distributions of property are made whenever a name is changed, a marriage contracted, a dance given, a copper sold, or, failing any such occasion, whenever a man accumulates a considerable amount of property and wishes to do something for the honor of his name and position. There is no word in the language of the Kwakiutl corresponding to our adopted word potlatch; but instead the various forms of the distribution have specific names. Making the promise to give a potlatch is *paqinuq* (*paqum*, having an angry, determined face), the word referring to the feeling, and consequent facial expression, which a man wears when he has determined to 'make his name high.' The giving of a single blanket (that is, half of a double blanket), or its value of twenty-five cents, to each person is called . . . 'spread open' because the blanket is spread out and held up as the name of each recipient is announced.

It should here be explained that the unit of value is the white woollen blanket with blue bars at the ends, originally obtained from the Hudson's Bay Company at seven dollars and fifty cents a pair. The value has steadily declined, until now a double

blanket is worth one dollar; but values are always given in terms of single blankets at fifty cents each, even though the amount be paid in double blankets, in other commodities, or in money. From former times has been inherited a quantity of blankets torn in halves, which now pass current at twenty-five cents each.

The giving of one or two double blankets to each person is *pasa* ('to flatten a basket'). *Mahwa* is the distribution of ten double blankets to each chief and smaller amounts to the others. *Walas sila* ('great around' the world) is the name of the great potlatch to which all the Kwakiutl tribes of a given district are invited.

In each gens is an hereditary official *takumi* ('holding the upper part'), who holds up each blanket or other gift before the assembly and presents it to the proper person. This is a position of great honor and responsibility, for as the gifts are distributed in the order of the comparative rank of the recipients, the decision of the *takumi* in cases of disputed rank may swing the balance of favor one way or the other. Quarrels and fights are of frequent occurrence at such times, when a man or his wife may snatch the blanket from the hands of the *takumi* in order to prevent the rival from obtaining it.

It has been said of the potlatch that 'the underlying principle is that of the interest-bearing investment of property.' This is impossible. A Kwakiutl would subject himself to ridicule by demanding interest when he received a gift in requital of one of like amount made by him. Not infrequently at a potlatch a guest calls attention to the fact that he is not receiving as much as he in his last potlatch gave the present host; and he refuses to accept anything less than the proper amount. Even this action is likened to 'cutting off one's own head,' and results in loss of prestige; for the exhibition of greed for property is not the part of a chief: on the contrary he must show his utter disregard for it. But to demand interest on a potlatch gift is unheard of. Furthermore, a man can never receive through the potlatch as much as he disburses, for the simple reason that many to whom he gives will die before they have a potlatch, and others are too poor to return what he gives them. Thus, only a chief of great wealth can make a distribution in which all the tribes participate and every person receives something; but all except a very few of these members of other tribes will never hold an intertribal potlatch, and consequently the man who gives presents to them cannot possibly receive any return from them. As to those who die, it may be said that theoretically a man's heir assumes his obligations, but he cannot be forced to do so, and if they far exceed the credits he is likely to repudiate them.

The potlatch and the lending of property at interest are two entirely distinct proceedings. Property distributed in a potlatch is freely given, bears no interest, cannot be collected on demand, and need not be paid at all if the one who received it does not for any reason wish to requite the gift. When the recipient holds a potlatch he may return an equal amount, or a slightly larger amount, or a smaller amount with perhaps the promise to give more at a future time.

The feeling at the bottom of the potlatch is one of pride, rather than greed. Occasionally men have tried to accumulate wealth by means of the potlatch and by lending at interest, but the peculiar economic system has always engulfed them, simply because a man can never draw out all his credits and keep the property thus acquired. Before his debtors will pay, he must first call the people together and inaugurate a potlatch, thus ensuring an immediate redistribution.

There are several rates of interest. Five pairs of blankets lent for about six months are repaid with six pairs, and this is called ... 'lend with'. *Tita* is interest at one hundred per cent on any amount from one pair to twenty, to be repaid in not less than one year, and perhaps—as when the debt is to be discharged at the time the lender must give a marriage dowry—not before the expiration of four or five years. ... 'Take hold of the foot' or ... 'sell a slave' is interest at two hundred per cent on a loan for an indefinite period of four or five years. A man requesting the loan of more than twenty pairs of blankets says, 'I wish you to take hold of the foot of my daughter'; or, 'I wish you to buy my daughter's name to be your slave.' The daughter of course is married, but her name is to be placed in pawn for the loan. If the prospective lender acquiesces he bids the other summon the people to witness the loan. The borrower takes a piece of cedar, and with his teeth splits off strips about the thickness of a match, which he breaks into lengths equal to the breadth of four fingers. Of these he makes three times as many as the blankets he is borrowing, ties them into a bunch, and gives it to the lender. A speaker cries out, 'Is that all you wish him to pay?' And the lender answers, 'That is all.' Thus the people take note of the contract.

There is constant borrowing at these exorbitant rates of interest. The explanation of the fact that the mass of the people have never found themselves bankrupt and the wealth of the tribe accumulated in the hands of a few men is that no one can compel payment of a debt without first showing good cause for the demand, and such cause can be found only in the expressed determination to perform some kind of public ceremony at which the property will be redistributed. Thus any property paid as principal and interest will revert quickly to the people; in fact, debts are paid only on the day of the distribution, so that practically no time elapses with the bulk of the tribal property in the hands of one man.

The destruction of canoes and the less common burning of blankets are [typical] other methods of showing disregard of the value of property with the aim of reflecting glory upon one's name. In the same category may be classed those feasts at which the prime endeavor is to squander more food than one's rival can equal in the feast which he must soon give in order to preserve his self-respect—to set before the guests so much that all cannot possibly be eaten, and the chiefs of the rival gens (or tribe), in their efforts to avoid the disgrace of leaving food and thus acknowledging the wealth and power of their host, may incur lasting disgrace by vomiting in the feast.

The greatest, because the most costly, of all feasts is the so-called 'grease' feast, in which a dish of oulachon oil is served to each guest, while huge quantities are thrown upon the fire with the purpose not only to destroy property but in so doing to cause such an intense heat that the host's rivals may be made to shrink from his fire. They on their part must not show any sign of discomfort, lest he at once compose a song of ridicule which would live into future generations to the dishonor of their descendants.

In every feast involving rivalry, the host has two objects in view: to destroy a great quantity of food, and to find or create some circumstance on which to base a taunting song.

X(1915), 141–144, 153

Hopi Traditionalism

When the government representative at the Navaho agency at Fort Defiance began to persuade the Hopi to take up modern methods of farming, Tuvi, an Oraibi man, was one of the few to fall in with his plans. But the chief, Lololma, was opposed to the new order of things, and the two quarrelled. The chief said, 'If you are going to follow the white man's ways, I do not want you to stay here.' So Tuvi took his wife and went to Provo, Utah, where he was baptized by the Mormons. After some years, about 1880, he returned and built a house at Moenkapi, and a few Oraibi families joined him. He afterward moved back to Oraibi, where he died, and the other families followed him. Later an old woman, Nasilewi, took possession of his Moenkapi house, and the other families returned from Oraibi. There are now about eighteen houses in the village. The name of Tuvi is the original of 'Tuba', the settlement near by, formerly occupied by Mormons, now the seat of a government school.

The Hopi reservation was established in 1882, but until the beginning of the twentieth century the people were practically independent of governmental authority. Since that time official supervision, assistance, and sometimes blundering interference in harmless religious and personal customs (witness a futile decree that Hopi men must wear the hair short), have become more and more effective, and the result is a gradual abandonment of the old order. In 1906 not a maid at East mesa but scrupulously kept her hair in the picturesque squash-blossom whorls indicative of the unmarried state. In 1912 the change in this single respect was

startling. Many saw no indecorum in allowing their locks to hang loosely. More and more the people are permanently taking up their residence in detached houses in the valleys. They are closer to their fields and sheep ranges, and so the change is a material gain; but it needs no prophet to foretell the eventual and probably not distant abandonment of the pueblos. And when that time

36 These Hopi girls at the trysting place wear the 'squash blossom' hair style traditional for unmarried women

arrives, the ancient ceremonies and home customs of the Hopi will be only a memory.

Nor is it difficult to predict what will be the last stronghold of Hopi culture. For some years prior to 1906 there was a gradually widening rift between two factions at Oraibi, the conservative and the liberal. The determination of government officials to enforce education crystallized sentiment, and the party that favored active resistance to restraint packed up their goods and chattels, marched forth from the pueblo, and built the new village Hotavila about four miles distant. Here they live with only the unavoidable minimum of contact with the white race, whom they unostentatiously but cordially hate. For them a few officious zealots are the American people. Their chief, recently released after a prison term of several years, during which no doubt he had abundant time to ponder on the futility of a Hopi insisting that his children be educated in his own ancient fashion when some individual two thousand miles away ordered him to cut their hair and deliver them at the schoolhouse, is a thoroughly embittered man, quiet in his bitterness, but unyielding. And that spirit pervades all his people. Henceforth they will formally obey orders, because they know of the force that lurks behind them, but many years will pass before they enter into the spirit of American education for their children. Meanwhile they cling to the old order. Desperately poor, they are diligent farmers, surpassing all other Hopi, and as they have more than enough of the best agricultural land on the reservation, lying on the mesa and adjacent to the village, and not in the distant valleys, there need be no apprehension as to their future. The pueblo is most unattractive. Few of the houses rise above a single story, and there is a rather disheartening air of newness.

On the same mesa and about a mile from Hotavila is Pakavi, which was established by another Oraibi faction a few years after the founding of Hotavila. The houses are all of one story and are ranged along both sides of a single street. The inhabitants are less morose than their neighbors, and while the village, in its exterior, resembles a Mexican settlement rather than a Hopi pueblo, it has an appearance of order and neatness in distinct contrast to Hotavila.

Deserted by these two factions, and by many families who have built houses at different places in the valley, Oraibi is practically an abandoned village.

XII(1922), 14–16

6 Social Customs

Social Customs of the Zuñi

Houses, though built by the men, are the absolute property of the women, who may sell or trade them within the tribe without legal hindrance from husband or children. Daughters are the preferred heirs of the landed possessions of their father and their mother, and sons are only heirs presumptive. Men obtain the use of land in their own right either by inheritance (when there are no sisters to claim it), or by occupying and cultivating unused community ground, or by purchase and exchange. The crops harvested from a man's land are stored in his wife's house, along with the yield of her own land. Personal property is divided among the children.

The attainment of puberty by girls is not always marked by prescribed behavior, inasmuch as marriage not infrequently occurs before that age. When an unmarried girl has her first period, her mother brings to the house either the paternal grandmother or a paternal aunt of the child. The older woman leads the girl to her home, where the child spends the day in vigorously grinding corn. The purpose of the practice is to insure ease of menstruation and to inculcate industrious habits.

When a man has obtained a girl's promise to marry, and she has secured the acquiescence of her parents, he goes with her to her house, where the mother bids the girl serve him with food. While he eats, she sits facing him, and the parents discourse on the duties of a husband. After spending five nights there, sleeping alone in a room apart from the family, he reports to his parents and soon returns to his bride with a new dress given by his mother. The girl now prepares a quantity of meal, and on the next day with a basket of it on her head she accompanies her husband to his parents' home. She partakes lightly of food placed before her by the mother-in-law, and the father-in-law gives her a deerskin for new moccasins. Together the couple repair to the bride's home, the girl carrying on her head a basket of wheat given by her mother-in-law, with the folded deerskin spread over it.

A pregnant woman must not look on a dead person, nor sprinkle water on a fire, lest her child have convulsions and sore ears and eyes. She must not roast food, nor steal, nor lie. She must not cohabit, even with her husband, or the child will be bald. There are no restrictions as to food. Her husband must not kill a snake. Some men refuse to kill anything; others, when they go rabbit-hunting, take some of the blood of each animal killed, and after the birth of the child the blood is mixed with water, which is rubbed over the infant's body and given it to drink. The father must not steal, or the child will have discharges at the ears and sores on the face.

Certain herbs are employed to prevent conception, and abortion is accomplished by pressing on the abdomen. After miscarriage a woman lies ten days face downward on a bed of sand covering a layer of hot stones, drinking quantities of hot water containing herbs and roots.

In parturition the woman lies on her back. A midwife aids the labor-pains by rubbing and pressing on the abdomen. In cases of delayed delivery the head-men of the Big Fire Society of shamans are summoned, and they shake their rattles, sing, and give the woman hot drinks and a cigarette of native tobacco wrapped in corn-husk. This is said to be infallibly successful in causing the expulsion of the child. The effect of the warm drinks in expanding the muscles and the nausea of the tobacco probably have a good effect.

When a child is about to be born, a woman well known as the mother of many healthy children is summoned to sit up all night with the expectant mother. As soon as the child is delivered, this godmother receives it, in order to impart good luck and long life. If the infant is a male, cold water is poured over the generative organ in order to forestall over-development, an act of kindness for his future wife. If it is a female, a new gourd is split in halves, and the open side of one half is rubbed over the vulva in order to enlarge the organ. The child is then wrapped in cloth and lashed to a cradle-board provided with three wooden hoops, which can be covered to protect the head from sun and flies, and women of the family prepare a bed of sand over heated stones, on which the mother and her infant lie for ten days. The heat is renewed as often as may be necessary.

The placenta is wrapped up and secretly buried, for if an animal should devour it the woman would lose her life. The navel-cord is severed with a knife, and the stump is covered with a pad of wool on which is placed a mixture of ground squash-seeds, piñon-gum, garlic, and fossil bivalves. When after several days the stump sloughs off, the father of a male infant buries it and the pad in a wooded place in the hills, and the mother of a female buries these objects beneath the floor behind the mealing-stones. This is to give the boy success at hunting and the girl a liking for the labor of grinding meal.

A name is chosen or invented for a newborn child by members

of the family. At dawn on the tenth day the mother or other female relative of the infant's mother takes it outside, holds it up just as the sun appears, and casts sacred meal toward the orb, begging long life for the child. She brings it back into the house, and they wash its head with soap-plant and its body with cold water. Then they bathe the mother in the same way.

During the day the godmother comes to bid the woman be ready at dawn on the next day. Before daylight therefore she is dressed and sits waiting, holding the child in her arms. The god-mother comes and stands outside the door, and just before the sun comes up she calls out: 'Siyotiwa [for example], come out! I want to see you!' The mother opens the door and gives her the infant, and the godmother holds him up to the sun, repeats the name, offers meal, and prays for his health and long life.

All boys at about the age of puberty are initiated into the Katikyanne ('god fraternity'), and thereafter they are capable of participating in the masked dances in which the gods are represented. There is no corresponding occasion in the life of Zuñi girls.

An unmarried youth ambitious to become a good hunter climbs the difficult trail to the base of the two conspicuous columns on the western side of Corn mountain. These represent the son and the daughter of the Corn Chief who sacrificed them to the angry watergod in order to check a deluge. Pointing an arrow at a cleft in the column representing the chief's son, he prays, with drawn bow, for good luck, and releases the arrow. If it sticks in the cleft, he knows that his arrow and his prayer have reached the heart of the sacrificed youth. If it fails, he tries as many as three times more. Whether successful or not, he may make the pilgrimage again and again.

An unmarried girl secures clay from the top of Corn mountain, makes a miniature pot, fills it with meal ground by herself, and places it at the base of the column representing the chief's daughter. This is to make her prolific and industrious. If a girl is too lazy to undertake the arduous trail, her father may bring a bit of sandstone from either of the columns, and she grinds it and drinks water in which the dust is stirred. Her children will be male or female according as the sandstone came from the 'boy' or the 'girl' column. There are several places where stones resembling female or male organs are put to a similar use.

When a Zuñi dies, the members of the clan and of the spouse's clan are immediately notified, and with other relatives and friends and his fraternity godfather they quickly assemble in the house. Even while the body is being prepared, female mourners begin to enter and set up a disheartening wail. The corpse is stretched out with the feet to the west. It is washed with soap-plant suds, dusted with meal, and clothed in fine garments, each of which is cut in order that its spirit may emerge and clothe the ghost. Then, wrapped in a blanket, the body is carried to the grave and interred with the head toward the east. For a very long time burial has been made in the little churchyard of the dilapidated and disused structure in the centre of the pueblo, the females on the north and the males on the south side, until now after thousands of bodies have been deposited there, bones are unearthed close to the surface whenever a grave is dug.

It is believed that the spirit lies lifeless four days after the burial. Then on the fifth morning it arises and goes to Ka-hluala-wa ('god village at'), in the sacred lake near St. Johns, Arizona, the reputed home of the Kakka ('gods'). There, and in all other lakes, springs, and rivers, the shadow people dwell.

XVII(1926), 107–110

The Naming and Cradling of Wichita Children

Children were named at birth, and sometimes before birth, after a bird, an animal, a dream, a vision, a dance, game, or what not, or it might be a name handed down in the family. As an illustration, when a woman gave birth, one of the women present by chance opened a door and saw the snow falling, so the child was named Natskiwus ('Snowbird'). If a child had good health it retained the birth name, though if the mother deemed it advisable she went to some man who had enjoyed good luck all his days and invited him to a feast. After eating, which included a ceremony of prayer and blessing, he would ask the woman what she wanted of him, and she responded that she desired a name for her child. After receiving food and being asked a favor, the man could not refuse the request, so he would give the child a name. A woman once dreamed that she had entered a house in the other world and that she had been asked to sit down where the spirits were telling stories. From this dream she gave her grandson a new

name, . . . 'Listening To The Party'. A man could assume a name from some good deed performed in war or in the chase. For instance, a chief had a son, to whom at birth was given the name . . . 'All Red Like The Indian People'. After the son grew up, he received a new name from an old man who had once brought in two prisoners. This new name was . . . 'Brought In To Be Killed'.

The making of the cradle for a child was attended with much care. The father was sent to the woods to gather the needed slender willow withes for the cradle frame. On finding the desired tree, he addressed it as though it were a person: 'You are the willow; you grow by the water; you are like the water. I have come to take your life; you will forgive me, for you are to be used for a cradle for my child.'

In cutting the osiers, the usual observance of the cardinal points was followed. The father peeled the sticks to be used, and the bark and shavings were carefully hidden lest they fall into the hands of witches.

To make the cradle, the father selected some woman of good health who knew the lore of the moon. The making was attended by an invocation to Kinnikasus and the Spirit of the Moon, that it might be well made and that the child might have good health and grow fast.

XIX(1930), 40–41

Child Rearing Customs of Coastal Salish Peoples

Immediately after the bathing of a newly born infant it was laid on its back on a cradle-board and a pad of furs, moss, or shredded cedar-bark was placed on the forehead and lashed to the opposite edges of the board, so that a constant, gentle pressure was applied to the soft bones of the infant's skull. In this position the child was kept during the first six months of its existence, except when it was removed for dressing. The broad, sloping forehead was an essential feature of beauty, and the face was regarded as handsome in direct proportion to the degree of slant. Early observers unite in declaring that the infants apparently suffered no pain, although they were less lively than unconfined children; and that the compression of the skull did not weaken the mentality. The custom of head-flattening began to grow obsolete with the arrival of traders, missionaries, and settlers, all of whom discouraged the practice; but it is never difficult to find among the old people evidences of this once invariable custom.

The ears of all children at the age of a few months are pierced without formality by old female relatives.

Personal names in this North Pacific region seldom have a translatable meaning. They are very ancient patronymics whose significance, if they ever possessed any, has been lost in the misty past.

It is the Cowichan custom to name a child as soon as it is able to walk. The father invites as many people as his means permit,

and when they have assembled in front of his house a man engaged by the father announces the name by which the child will be known. This is nearly always the name of an ancestor or a living relation. Money is then distributed, fifty cents to each person, Formerly of course the gifts were articles of native manufacture. When a youth or a favorite daughter reaches maturity, the father again calls the people to his house and announces a new name, which is retained until death. For the

Cowichan have not the habit common to most Salish tribes of the coast: namely, that of changing the name whenever a beloved relative or friend dies, lest the sound of those names so often uttered by the lost loved one bring a constant reminder of sorrow.

On Puget sound a young child is referred to as the youngest or the eldest, or by a sobriquet based on some salient characteristic or adventitious circumstance. He is not formally named before the age of six or even twelve years, and invariably the name then bestowed is that of some deceased relative, especially one of note. New names are never invented for children. The delay in applying formal names is based on two grounds. First, it is desired to see whom the child may grow to resemble, in order that he may perpetuate the name as well as the form of that person. Secondly, they wish to be certain that the child will be robust and will live, so that the name of some illustrious ancestor be not wasted on him; for the names of the dead are not uttered for many years after death, until time has dulled the fang of grief. If an infant were named after an ancestor and then died in childhood, the name could not be revived again for about ten years more, and its likelihood of being perpetuated would thus be lessened.

The birth of twins is regarded as a calamity, or at least a threatened calamity, for the entire band. There is some occult, undefined connection, it is believed, between twins and the salmon, and the result of this connection, it is thought, is that unless there is immediate purification and expiation by the parents of the infants, the salmon, as well as other fish that run in schools, will not come to the shores that season. In former times, therefore, as soon as the news of such an event went abroad, the relatives of the parents hurried to the house and completely stripped it of its contents, each claiming and holding as his own whatever he carried away; and the parents carried their twin babies away into the woods at the head of some stream or to the shore of some lake. There they remained for a year, touching no fish nor flesh, but subsisting on roots, sprouts, and berries. Morning and evening they bathed in the stream or the lake, and frequently they fasted and sought visions in order to gain the aid of the supernaturals. Since the twin children were the occasion of disgrace and hardship, there was no reason for caring whether they lived or died, or for doing more than to protect them from death by starvation or exposure; so the little ones were allowed to crawl about at will, and to cry their hearts out unheeded. If they survived the hardships and returned with their parents, they had proved their worth and were ever after accepted as normal individuals. The parents, too, having purified themselves and warded off tribal disaster, returned to their ordinary mode of living, not only absolved from all blame, but freed, as they thought, from the possibility of again bearing twins.

Children were taught to obey their parents, to respect the

aged, to be silent in the presence of their elders, and to show kindness toward their fellows. At eight they learned to swim, and at twelve years of age boys were trained in the use of weapons and the instruments of the chase, while girls began to learn basketry, weaving, and the duties of the household.

Customs attendant upon the arrival of girls at puberty were basically uniform, yet in detail they showed enough diversity to justify the description of several variations. The principles involved are two. First, it is believed that at such a time a girl is unclean, and must be segregated from the rest of the family. For the same reason there are certain things she must not eat, lest the supply of those particular foods fail. Secondly, it is thought that the conduct of the maiden at this period determines the moral character and to a large extent the physical wellbeing of the mature woman. All girls, therefore, as soon as they became pubescent, were placed apart during the catamenial period; but only in the case of a maiden of rank did the observance become a festival.

The Cowichan are the only ones who still observe these practices. . . . The girl is made to sit on a pile of blankets on the bed at the rear of the room, where, naked except for a girdle of goat-hair fringe and with face powdered with red pigment, she remains for four days, working constantly at basketry. She eats and drinks practically nothing, must not touch fresh fish nor fresh meat, nor scratch with the fingers but with a stick. At sunrise and at sunset the women of the village are called in and sit about the room, beating with sticks on poles or boards, and singing certain songs pertaining to this occasion, while two of them place themselves on either side of the girl and shake their rattles. Men take no part, but are not prohibited from entering the house to look on. At the end of four days the father distributes blankets among the women for their services in singing, and an old woman takes the girl away from the village to bathe. The reason for keeping the girl confined at this period of her life is that she may always be reserved and not wanton. She is denied food and drink in order that she may be hardy and able to endure hunger and thirst when necessary. Here and elsewhere the custom is observed only in the better families. If on the first day, as used to happen, a young man should enter the house and sit down beside the girl, this would signify his desire to marry her; and so sacred was this custom that the father seldom made any objection, no matter what his personal feeling toward the young man might be, always providing, of course, that no youth of lower station attempted to climb the social ladder by this route. During the four days the young man would sit beside the girl, sharing her fast and her silence, and at the end of that time he, instead of the father, distributed blankets, and the marriage was thus consummated.

A Songish girl was sent by her parents to a little conical wickiup of poles and mats on the edge of the village, where she remained in solitude for five days, observing the usual taboos against scratching with the fingers or eating fresh fish or fresh meat. On the fifth day the friends and relatives and many spectators assembled at the hut, and two young men brought a large basket filled with water. The pair danced about it for a while in a jocular manner, and then surrendered it to five chosen women, who carried it into the wickiup and bathed the girl. Dressed in fresh clothing, she emerged with her attendants, and a merry feast was enjoyed, after which presents were distributed by the father. For a few days following she washed her face twice daily with water and a bunch of soft, shredded cedarbark, in order to preserve her beauty. A stone depended from the ends of her hair, in order to cause it to grow long, and she anointed it with certain plant juices to make it glossy.

The Clallam custom compelled a girl to disrobe and sit naked in one corner of the house for five days, denying herself food and drink except in very small quantities. At night, attended by her mother, she bathed in a stream or a bay, rubbing the body with the tips of hemlock boughs. The woman assisted, rubbing and moulding the limbs as if to make them shapely.

Everywhere a mature girl was carefully watched and guided by her parents. The boys however were free from restraint. If a girl became hopelessly lax in her morals, she was usually disowned by her parents as valueless, since no man would purchase such a woman for his wife. But this does not mean that she was doomed to a life of prostitution. On the contrary her chances of marriage were excellent, although she could not expect the honor of being bought; and if after marriage she proved reasonably faithful to her spouse, public opinion soon forgot, or at least ceased to discuss, her misdemeanors. It must be remembered that sexual freedom was not looked upon as a moral wrong; simply, a loose woman cheapened herself, and, if married, exposed her husband to ridicule. Among families of high rank a girl's first error sometimes caused a bloody feud, but more frequently she was married to her lover.

Boys also celebrated their attainment of puberty by a form of purification. The Cowichan tribes still observe this custom. When a boy's changing voice indicates that he has reached the age of puberty, an old man sends him out early in the morning on four successive days to bathe in a stream, or preferably a lake, apart from the village, and to take a handful of spruce twigs and rub his breasts violently, so as to break the skin and cause bleeding, lest his breasts continue to swell and attain the size of a woman's. Sometimes rough pieces of stone instead of spruce needles are used. This is repeated in the evening, but the day is spent in the house, little food and drink being taken.

From this time on to young manhood, and in many cases beginning years before puberty, the boys of all tribes were sent at intervals to make journeys, first short, but gradually increasing in length and difficulty, in the belief that among the distant mountains or in the mysterious depths of the dark forests the traveller might perchance encounter some spirit which would take pity on him and become his lifelong guardian. Storms and the hour of dusk were regarded as most probable seasons for the spirits to be abroad, and sometimes even physical punishment was necessary to drive the fear-stricken child out into the dreaded solitudes.   IX(1913), 80–85

Child Rearing Practices of Nootkan Peoples

Among the Nootkan tribes a newly born child was bathed in

warm water, anointed with dogfish oil, especially about the eyes, and wrapped in shredded cedar-bark. A piece of partially dried blubber was given it to suck until the mother's flow of milk was satisfactory, and the mother herself ate more than the usual quantity of blubber in order to enrich her milk. The infant was bathed daily, and on the fifth day, still wrapped in bark fibre, it was placed in the woven bark carrier with a pad of bark laced tightly over the forehead and other pads at the sides of the head to prevent the head from turning and from bulging out at the sides. As it grew older it was taken out of the carrier when not sleeping, and at the age of about eighteen months the carrier was dispensed with. The following is a Hesquiat mother's lullaby sung to her boy baby:

Who is that child passing, hair blown by the wind, fishing?
Caught only one with your hook, you fish-line boy.
Who is that child passing?

At a very early age a boy began to receive instruction from his grandfather in hunting, fishing, and rules of conduct under various circumstances. Girls were taught by their grandmothers. Children were allowed to do much as they pleased, and were seldom punished.

XI(1916), 40–41

Apsaroke Child Rearing Customs

When a boy was just old enough to walk, the father sometimes caught a young snowbird, and told the child in the presence of his clansmen to strike it with his stick. If the little fellow struck a sharp blow, killing the bird, it was regarded as a sign that he would become a great hunter and warrior, and the father gave his clansmen presents so that they would speak praises of the child and make prayer and prophecy that it would have long life.

At a very early age the boy was put into a small saddle, but not tied, and being young and foolish he would whip the horse to make him run, which of course resulted in his being thrown. At twelve years he could ride spirited horses like a man. In summer the father took him into deep water, and standing a short distance away told him to swim to him; the child paddled manfully, but usually sank before reaching his father. This practice, however, soon made the boy an accomplished swimmer, who could cross broad rivers back and forth without resting.

At about the age of seven the youngster was given a small bow and taught how to hold and shoot blunt arrows at a thick braid of grass, which gradually was moved farther away. As he became skilful he was told to go out and try to kill little birds. When he could kill rabbits, points were fixed to his arrow-shafts, and he

42 *Apsaroke Youths*

was taken out to learn how to kill buffalo. His father filled a small quiver with arrows for him, mounted him on a swift but safe horse, and when the chase began directed him to a calf, into which, if the first arrow failed to bring it down, the boy sent shaft after shaft. Then the father in his pride gave the horse to one of his clansmen. After he had shot a few calves without assistance, the eager young hunter was allowed to chase full-grown buffalo.

At fourteen or fifteen he was urged to go into the hills and fast while he was yet continent, that the spirits might come to him and give him of their strength, since now he must join the men on their hunts and in their war-raids. When the youth was first sent out with a war-party, the father asked a relative to watch over him, and if the party returned victorious, the clansmen of the father gathered about his lodge in a great semicircle, dancing and singing praises of the youth; and the father gave them all presents, until at times he had no property left.

Boys of twelve to fifteen organized societies in imitation of those of the men, making a drum and four staffs decorated with eagle back-feathers, which were given to the four recognized leaders of the band. Their enemies were the coyotes and wolves, and when the tribe was on the move, their mounted band would scour the prairies in search of these animals. If one succeeded in striking an 'enemy', it was counted a coup, and at evening when the fires were being lighted in the camp, they would come charging in just like a returning war-party.

In summer when the weather was hot and the camp was filled with drying meat, the boys would leave their clothing at the river-side and smear themselves from head to foot with blue clay. Then with sticks they would charge upon the camp, each one singing the song of some noted warrior, sometimes even his sacred medicine-song. They ran through the camp snatching meat wherever they could, and as they numbered from twenty to forty they took away a good supply for the feast. The women ran out and threw old scraps of meat and rubbish at them, and gave chase for a time; but there was no anger, as the custom was a recognized one. Returning to the woods where one of their number had been left to build a fire, they roasted their meat, piled it on cottonwood leaves, and sat around it in a circle. One of their number was called forth to sit in front as the greatest man among them.

Young girls had miniature lodges about four feet high, made of buffalo calf-skins, and arranged inside with beds and utensils as in the living lodges. There they played a great deal, pretending to be grown-up women with husbands, much as white children do. On short marches they dragged the small poles for their tipis, and at the end of the day pitched them as did their mothers.

The young girl was in the care of her grandmother, who would speak to her in this fashion: 'Look at your brothers; they are poor. Try to live so that some one will love you and buy you. When women are taken from their husbands by other men it is not good.' Training in household duties began at an early age, and by the time the girl was fourteen she could tan skins and was beginning to make clothing. At that age mothers kept a watchful eye over their daughters, and began to accompany them whenever they went on errands such as fetching water, carrying wood, or going to the meadows to gather hay for the horses.

In winter the girls coasted down the snow-clad hills on sleds of buffalo-ribs covered with rawhide; and the boys, having none, would leap on behind the girls and ride down with them. When the ice was smooth, it was crowded with children and youths using buffalo-skulls for sleighs. The skull was drawn on its face by a rope tied through the nose; at the back a stick was fastened through the orifice of the spine, and grasping this, perched on a folded robe, the girls were drawn swiftly over the ice by the boys and young men.

Tiring of this, they formed in large circles, boys and girls, each with the arms about the shoulders of the one in front, and so danced around in a circle, swaying from side to side. The participants were mostly unmarried persons, but sometimes a young married woman would slip out and join in the dance.　　IV(1909), 26–29

Coastal Salish Games

Forms of amusement were numerous. Shinny was much played by mixed parties, but mostly by women. The ball was usually of yew, and about three or four inches in diameter.

The very common hoop-and-pole game was current in this region. The hoop, about six inches in diameter, was rolled swiftly toward the contestants, who with their spears stood waiting thirty or forty feet away and endeavored to hurl their　　43 *A Point of Interest—Navaho*

shafts through it in such a manner that the spear would transfix the turf and hold the hoop. Bows and arrows sometimes took the place of spears. Shooting arrows at a mark was much practised. But none of these contests were held during the salmon spawning season, for the invisible spirits of the salmon, passing through the village on their way up stream, might be struck by a missile and become angered, not to return that way again.

A game affording a deal of fun was that known as 'make you laugh.' The players, old and young, divided into two groups, males in one and females in the other. Between the two parties two slender sticks were thrust into the ground, and it was the endeavor of the players to march from their line, one by one, to the sticks and back without smiling, halting long enough at the centre to look slowly along the line of opposing faces. From that line came a volley of jeers and jokes intended to force a smile from the contestant, and any who could refrain from smiling scored a point for his side. At this game the girls and women usually won.

In summer children enjoyed getting into the stream or the bay and splashing water into one another's faces, those of opposite sex forming opposing lines and each endeavoring to force the other to retreat.

An indoor winter game much played by the young people in mixed companies was known in the Nisqualli dialect as *sadak*. After the players had been equally divided, one from each side squatted on his heels, and without rising hitched and hopped about on his toes as long as he could. As fast as one dropped out, another from his side took up the contest. A strong, practised dancer would tire out several opponents, and the party that excelled in endurance won the game.

IX(1913), 95   Foot races, canoe races, and swimming contests were frequent.

Hopi Games and Running

'Corncob kicking' (*Sono-wunpa*) is a contest between men of the same kiva. In winter-time the men gather in their respective kivas to pass the time in spinning yarn, weaving cloth, and telling stories; and to break the monotony they sometimes divide into two parties and choose leaders, each side providing itself with a *sono*, a bunch of four corncobs to which a cord is attached in such manner that there is left a loop into which the toes fit snugly. One *sono* is black, the other white. Then the two leaders lie on their backs at the foot of the kiva ladder with their heads toward the fireplace and attempt to fling their *sono* up through the hatchway. Usually many attempts are necessary before success is attained. When a missile goes flying out through the hatchway, those to whom it belongs rush after it, and the first one to reach it throws himself down on his back and kicks it over his head toward the beginning of the Stairway trail. In this fashion the two parties race down the trail, around Tawa-pa spring at the foot of the trail, and back into the kiva. It occasionally happens that on the return a *sono* is accidentally flung over the edge of the cliff, and it must then be recovered and brought back in the usual way. Before the start they roll balls of blue cornmeal about small pebbles, making them the size of the fist, and place them in the fire to bake, and these 'round piki' are claimed by the winners.

The 'kicking race' . . . is a contest between the members of the different kivas, and is held only in the spring. Each kiva has a ball somewhat smaller than the fist and made of stone, piñon-gum, or a micaceous mineral that has been calcined, powdered, mixed with urine, and formed into a ball before it hardens. The leaders of the respective parties take position near the foot of the western trail that descends from the Gap, and the other runners spread out ahead of them. At a signal the leaders throw the ball forward by means of the bare foot, and the other contestants run after the missiles, each party kicking its own ball forward along a course that encircles the southern end of the mesa, crosses the valley eastward as far as the wash, follows the wash to the Keams Canyon road, turns westward along the road, and mounts the trail past the ruin Kisakobi to the first terrace. The distance is said to be about six miles. There is no ceremonial significance in the contest, which is merely a trial of endurance and fleetness between the members of the five kivas. Sometimes this race is run over a course of about fifteen miles, starting at the same place, but proceeding to the foot of the mesa that lies to the northwest, then southward to the arroyo between East and Middle mesas, to the foothills southeast of Walpi, northward to the Keams Canyon road, and back toward the village and up the trail to the first terrace. In these days few of those who enter the race are able to finish the course.

One hears remarkable stories about Hopi distance running, such, for example, as that familiar one of the man who used to run forty miles to his cornfield, hoe it, and return home for a late breakfast! But there is no doubt that the Hopi of former generations were stout-hearted runners. Letayu, now an old man, avers without apparent pride or boastfulness that he once carried an official letter from Keams Canyon to Fort Wingate in two days, spending the first night at Fort Defiance. On the third morning he left Fort Wingate before 'gray dawn' and arrived at Fort Defiance before sunrise. Setting out again at sunrise, he reached Keams Canyon a little after mid-afternoon. The air-line distances involved are: Keams Canyon to Defiance, sixty-three miles; Defiance to Fort Wingate, thirty-eight miles.

44 *Sticks Used in the Hupa Guessing Game*

XII(1922), 51–52

Hupa: The Guessing Game

The Hupa have only a few games. The guessing contest played by men is called *kin* ('stick'). Each of two players has about one hundred very thin, round sticks, one of which is distinguished by a black band. These are obtained in the mountains, in order that they may be lucky. A player puts his hands behind his back and separates the sticks into two lots, brings them foward, and holds them beside his thighs, while his backers beside and behind him, who have wagered their valuables on his success, beat a drum and sing. The other studies his opponent's face, then suddenly claps his hands and makes a gesture indicating which hand, in his opinion, contains the black-banded stick. If the guess is successful, the inning passes to him; but if unsuccessful, the player takes from the space between them one of twelve tally-sticks. The entire number of sticks must be in possession of one player or the other, in order to decide a wager. When a player has ten of them, the 'dealer' announces, ... 'two left!' Then a successful play on his part concludes the game.

Nootkan Courting Customs

Courting was done secretly. It was rather difficult to meet alone a girl of high birth, but to exchange whispered words and tokens in the night through the cracks in the wall was a simple matter; and if the suitor possessed the courage he could occasionally creep through the door and into his sweetheart's presence. Parents were inclined to wink at the peccadilloes of their daughters—and in this category the North Pacific tribes placed all the major sins—provided only the manner of the doing were not too overt. The girl who was trained to be so circumspect in the street that she would not lift an eye from the ground, who never left the village except in the company of her mother or a slave woman, that same damsel might in the dead of night receive more than one secret lover in her bedroom. But that was nothing to her discredit, so long as she maintained her circumspectness in public. An interesting commentary on this phase of Nootka life is presented in the following song, which was composed and made public by a man who overheard a young woman boasting to another that the married women were jealous and afraid of her because she had no husband.

'I am the one, husbandless, whom the married women fear,' she said, Talking foolishly, as if she were drunken.

XI(1916), 65–66

Hupa Sexual Customs

... [A]ll men and boys slept in the sweat-house. This applies to married men as well as to bachelors. The permanent houses however were occupied for only a few months in the winter, and with the coming of clement weather everybody moved into camp along the streams or near the food preserves. This was regarded as the proper season for sexual intercourse, but generally it was only hunters and men of great self-control who, under the influence of religious taboos, strictly observed this rule. For two

108

days after cohabitation men and women ate no meat, and during that time they ate their fish and acorn mush out of individual dishes, not from the common vessels. Nursing women did not indulge themselves, and a man who had many children of tender years became ashamed, and endeavored to remain apart from his wife for at least two years. Venison was never carried into the house through the door, because that was used by the people, and especially by women, and therefore to carry venison through it would have meant bad luck in hunting deer.

Marriages always occurred in the summer, for the reason that men and women slept in separate houses during the winter. Negotiations were carried on between two men representing the two families, and a payment of shell money was made at once to bind the girl's parents. Since most of the inhabitants of a village were related on the male side, the majority of marriages were between members of different villages. At the appointed time the bride's party set out in canoes laden with property of every kind, arriving at their destination in the evening in season to partake of the wedding feast. In return for their presents they received articles of equal value.

A considerable sum was paid for a girl of good family. However this custom may have originated, the Hupa in later times had not the feeling that the woman was actually purchased, like any article of commerce; the payment was made in order to give rank and dignity to the woman and her children. It was in fact a sign of formal marriage, as much so as our marriage license. When the bride-groom's relative carried to the bride's house the shell money and woodpecker-scalps composing the wedding payment, the people assembled to witness the transaction, and the woman's future standing depended on the amount. A woman for whom only a small amount was given was regarded as scarcely married at all; her husband lived in her house, and was called *honta-yechuwinya* ['house goes-into']. The woman treated him like a servant, ordering him hither and yon in the performance of menial labor. Those who lived together without the payment of anything at all were considered not to be married. The children of these 'half marriages' and illegitimate unions were dishonoured for life, and generally became slaves.

The bride's family kept intact the amount of her wedding gift until her first child was well grown. They were then permitted to do with it as they desired. If before that time the woman proved unfaithful and left her husband, they had to restore the property to his family. Thus the payment was a pledge for her good conduct.

XIII(1924), 19–20, 22–23

Miwok: Marriage and Taboos

Polygyny, though a recognized institution, was not of very common occurrence. A man had the first right to his brother's widow, but the privilege is said to have been rather rarely exercised. On the other hand, a widower was expected to take the unmarried sister of his deceased wife, and neglect of her in preference of another caused adverse comment. The wife's younger sister was a man's logical choice if he desired and could support two wives; he also had the right to these relatives of his wife: her brother's daughter, and her father's sister. Blood relatives could not marry, with one exception: a man and his mother's brother's daughter, that is, his first cousin. But this cousin is precisely the woman whom his father also has the right to marry, because she is his wife's brother's daughter. We thus have a situation where either a man or his son may properly marry a certain woman. Marriage of blood relatives is contrary to Indian feeling, and this contravention of custom [E. W.] Gifford ingeniously explains as probably the result of the father's passing on to the son his prior right to a woman whom he did not need.

This right of father and son to the same woman offers a possible solution of the widespread and unexplained taboo on conversation between a woman and her father-in-law, and

45 A Kwakiutl bridal group, the bride flanked by two professional dancers and the fathers of bride and groom

between a man and his mother-in-law. If the son married her, she became the daughter-in-law of a man who might have been her husband; and if he were seen conversing with her there very likely would have been a suspicion that he was arranging a clandestine meeting to claim the privileges that he had yielded to his son. Granting this origin of the taboo between a woman and her father-in-law, it is not difficult to imagine that the corresponding one between a man and his mother-in-law was simply a logical extension of the original taboo.

Among the Miwok the taboo on conversation, physical contact, and exchange of glances, applied not only to these two relationships, but also where the relationship was merely potential. Thus, it applied to a man's conduct toward his mother-in-law's sister, his mother's brother's wife, and his brother's mother-in-law, because any one of these might, according to custom, become, or at least might have been, his mother-in-law. For a similar reason it applied to a woman's relations toward her father-in-law's brother, and her sister's father-in-law.

XIV(1924), 140–141

Haida: Marriage Breakdown

If a man mistreated his wife, her parents had the right to reclaim her and the children. If he ran away and married another woman, he was made to pay indemnity, failing which he was liable to be shot. If however he simply abandoned his wife and took no other woman, there was no redress. Such separations were very common; in fact, marriages generally were of short duration. Payment could be forced from a man who abandoned a paramour in order to marry another woman; generally however the discarded one had not the audacity to make the demand. A widow was expected to marry a relative of her deceased husband, and if she refused, she was compelled to pay his family. Disputes over women were the most prolific source of strife. Death was not rarely the portion of a man who tampered with another's wife, even if she shared his guilt; for the injured husband, after fasting for several days, might suddenly attack his enemy in the street with a knife. More often he demanded indemnity. Inasmuch as the killing of a tribesman had to be satisfied by all the family of the murderer, the entire family of a wronged husband met in council to decide which course should be pursued. If the desire for revenge prevailed over prudence and thrift, and the adulterer was killed, they then had to carry valuable presents, even such as slaves and canoes, to the murdered man's family. But if the original killing of the adulterer were avenged in kind, then both families exchanged presents. Even after the payment of blood-money, some member of the murdered man's family might harbor a feeling of revenge, and kill some one of his enemies, and thus engender a lasting feud. Men have even killed their own nephews in disputes about women.

A man whose relative had been killed by a tribesman might decide that it was best not to take summary vengeance nor yet to make a direct demand for payment. With his sister, if he had one, he would go to the house of his relative's slayer, who, having been informed of what was to occur, had assembled his family. They received the two with rude treatment, and handled the man roughly and threateningly. The two, refusing to be intimidated, danced, and the family began to pile up blankets for them. The man danced with his eyes shut, and would not open them until he was satisfied with the amount given. So well established was this institution of wergild that even today, if the borrower of a canoe is drowned while using it, the owner must pay the family of the deceased: for if he had not lent the canoe, death could not have occurred. So it is with all weapons and implements. This is an interesting parallel with the old English common law in regard to deodands, by which any object that had been instrumental in causing death was confiscated for the king and supposedly applied to pious uses.

XI(1916), 121–122

Sexual Customs of the Western Woods Cree

If a man coveted a married woman sufficiently to pay a horse, a gun, or other article of like value, he would talk it over with her, and if she acquiesced he gave her the promised gift, which she brought to her husband. If he accepted it, by this act he took the other for *okusaka* ('his comrade'). Whenever the latter desired the woman's company, he notified the husband, who absented himself for the night. Presents of lesser value were given at intervals, and if the husband at any time especially needed some certain thing he despatched his wife to his comrade, who was bound to provide it if he had or could in any way procure it. Such an arrangement was made only when the woman was pleased with her proposed secondary husband.

When a man learned that his unmarried daughter was co-habiting with a man, he said nothing immediately, but if the relationship continued indefinitely he would become angry and declare: 'If you are going to keep this up, you will have to leave my tipi, or your lover will have to marry you. Go and talk to him, and see if he will pay for you.' He himself would not make overtures to the man.

Mother-in-law and son-in-law never address each other directly, but speak when necessary through the daughter and wife; and if the two chance to be in the same tipi together, they sit with bowed head or averted face. An instance is cited of a woman and her son-in-law left alone for a moment, when a birch-bark dish hanging in the tipi fell into the fire. Both simultaneously reached for it, and both recoiled. Both reached again, and again drew back; and so until it was too late to save the dish. Neither was willing to lay hand to it at the same time as the other. No explanation of the taboo is offered, though [it is recorded] hearsay that a woman's speaking to her son-in-law is a sure indication of her having conceived a criminal affection for him.

An adulterous wife was either 'thrown away,' perhaps with the loss of her nose, or flogged and retained. Sometimes after long separation a couple reconciled their differences and remarried. Combat with deadly weapons over women were not rare, especially in the times of the fur-traders, whose ambassador was 'fire water.'

XVIII(1928), 73–74

Mohave Mortuary Customs

Matevilye, before dying, instructed his people as to the disposition of his body. They were to dig a hole in the ground, put quantities of fuel over it, and when he was dead place his body on the top of all, kindle the pyre, and gather about to mourn and watch his departure to the after-world. And so they do with their dead to this day. Their god taught them what disposal to make of the body, and no missionary can divert them from this so-termed pagan practice. When it is certain that death is to come, the funeral pyre is prepared. As soon as life is extinct the body is wrapped in a blanket, carried out, and placed on the pyre.

46 *A Haida Chief's Tomb at Yan*

Relatives and friends follow the remains, all seemingly equally grief-stricken. In the language of the Indian, 'Why not? We are all brothers. When my brother is happy, I am happy with him. When he weeps, I weep with him.' So, gathered around the blazing pile, the tribe wails until corpse and fuel have been consumed, and the ashes have dropped into the pit below. Four days after the cremation the spirit goes to Nevthi Chuvachu, Spirit House, in Selyaita, the Sand Hills, along the Colorado south of Topock. This place of spirits they believe to be prolific in melons, beans, pumpkins, and game. When one melon is plucked from the vine, another immediately takes its place; when an ear of corn is picked, another shoots forth. Every Mohave who dies goes to this place, no matter how he has lived, whether bravely or cravenly. Even those who in life have wrought evil through sorcery are not debarred. No Mohave can be induced to tarry in that region—that world of departed spirits. If one were to sleep in Selyaita, the spirits of his relatives who have gone before would take his own spirit from him.

The names of the dead are never uttered. If a Mohave dies before his child has learned to speak, that child will never know what name its father bore. In this may be seen a potent reason for the weakness of this people in hunting and fighting. The custom of the Sioux, for example, of singing their babes to sleep with songs recounting the mighty deeds of great ancestors and of encouraging the boys to emulate their exploits, furnished notable incentive for attaining prowess in war and the chase.

II(1908), 52

7 Ceremonies

The Luiseno Girls' Puberty Rite

At the conclusion of their period of confinement in the heated pit the girls had their faces painted red, and circlets of hair were placed on their wrists and ankles, and bands of a certain plant about their heads. They wore these symbols for several months, and at the same time they abstained from meat, fish, and salt. The duration of this taboo was not fixed, but was left largely to the inclination of the individual. After their faces had been painted, the girls with their female attendants repaired to a large rock near the village, and painted on its surface certain geometric designs. At the end of each month for an indefinite period their faces were repainted in a different fashion, and new designs were added on the rock.

An important feature of the girls' puberty ceremony was connected with an earth mosaic. Some say it occurred a month after the dance; others, at the end of a year. A small hole was scooped out in the ground, and the material was heaped in a circle several feet in diameter, and within were represented various celestial bodies. With ashes, charcoal, and powdered red paint the enclosing circle and the periphery of the central hole were made black on the inside, red in the middle, and white on the outside. The figure represented the universe, and a northward opening in the circle the road the soul takes in its flight. Having completed this work, the officiating chief walked thrice around it, and with a pellet of pulverized chia and salt he touched various parts of the body of a girl and ended by placing it in her mouth. This he did to each girl. He then made a speech enjoining good conduct, and the girls, kneeling beside the earth picture, expelled the chia pellets into the central hole. Other old men at once destroyed the picture and buried the pellets by pushing the earth into the hole. The significance of the pellets apparently is no longer known, but the purpose of the rites as a whole was to promote the health and moral well-being of the girls, and particularly to insure fecundity and easy parturition.

XV(1926), 17–18

The Kutenai Bear Ceremony

The Kutenai observed a ceremony each spring for the purpose

of securing immunity from attack by the grizzly bear, who soon would be coming out of his winter quarters. Each participant wished him good luck during the summer and requested the same for himself. At the same time the hope was expressed that the grizzly-bear would not send sickness upon the people, and especially not upon the children of the suppliant.

The ceremony was under the direction of the man who first in the course of the year dreamed of the grizzly-bear. Immediately after his dream he went about the camp announcing that he would 'make the [Bear Ceremony]' in the spring. When that season arrived, he prepared the whitened-earth ellipse in his lodge, and just behind it laid a bear-skull, with the nose pointing toward the entrance. On each side of the skull he placed the skeletonized fore paw of a bear, the claws directed toward the front. The whole arrangement was designed to resemble the appearance of a bear lying at the mouth of a den with its head between its fore paws. Late in the day he went about the camp kicking the lodge-pole at the door of each lodge, and crying, 'Have you anything to give?' Whoever had a medicine-bundle then gave it to him, saying where he wished to have it placed, as, for instance, on a certain lodge-pole or in a certain position near the bear-skull. The dreamer carried all the medicine-bundles to his lodge and arranged them in the desired positions.

Then at nightfall the people came to his lodge, and each one, beginning with the one sitting at the left of the bear-skull, filled his pipe and gave smoke to the bear, praying: 'You are coming out in a few days, and I want you not to bite me, or my children, or my people. Do not make us sick. I want you to have a good summer, with good food, and may we have the same.'

After each person had voiced his supplication, the dreamer,

sitting behind the skull started the songs of the bear, which were equal in number to the claws on the altar, and the women arose to dance, making motions and uttering cries imitative of the bear. . . .

SONG OF THE MALE BEAR

It is my voice, Grizzly-bear; it is I, Grizzly-bear.

Then, beginning with the man at the left of the skull, each person sang his individual medicine-songs, the others assisting. At daybreak each departed with his medicine-bundle.

VII(1911), 140–143

Hidatsa: The Ceremony of the Bowl

In addition to the Sun Dance, the Hidatsa had two four-days ceremonies of supplication by ordeal in which the principal features were piercing and fasting. The more important of these was . . . Taking Up The Bowl, based on the legend of the sacred bowl, which symbolizes Old Woman Who Never Dies and figures so prominently in Hidatsa mythology.

According to the legend as passed down by the chief Road-maker, uncle of Lean Wolf, in the days when the [people] were encamped near a beautiful lake to the northeast, one of their young men was fasting on the shore far from the village, and crying to the spirits to pity him. Just before the sun went behind the world, he saw something on the shore where the waves

48 The Hopi, though it means little to them, join the Tewa immigrants of Hano in the Buffalo Dance

lapped the sand, and when he came closer he perceived that it was an earthen vessel marked with the track of a brant around its rim.

He took it to his lodge, for he thought it must be a vessel of mystery. That night he had a vision, and the bowl spoke to him in the words of a woman, saying, 'My child, I am Old Woman Who Never Dies. Hold me sacred, and I will bring you good fortune, for I have many friends among the spirits. The corn and the buffalo-paunch are my food. I shall teach you the songs and rites of a ceremony that will cause your people to prosper and bring rain upon your crops. Make offerings to me of buffalo-paunches, and hang them before me on cottonwood stakes. Prepare a pipe and tobacco for [my attendant spirits], for they are men and like the smoke. All the birds and animals living on this lake are of my medicine. Let no man who has blood on his hands enter the lodge where this ceremony takes place, nor permit any women to be present.'

Then she revealed to him the rites of Taking Up The Bowl.

A man who desired this ceremony performed climbed to the top of his earthen lodge and appealed to Old Woman Who Never Dies: 'Bowl, I cause you to be taken up, that my children may grow strong. Let the rain come upon us.' Or he might go to the hills and utter this prayer, crying like a child. Already he had provided offerings, and food, robes, and clothing.

When all was ready he sought the Keeper of the Bowl, and offered him the pipe, apprising him of the object of his visit. The Keeper told him that he was doing right to take up the bowl, and accepted the pipe, lighted it, and prayed to the sacred vessel, which was kept in the honor place of his lodge: 'Bowl, we are about to take you up again with prayers and fasting. Open your ears that you may hear our songs. Give us your aid.'

He silently repeated songs and prayers until the morning of the ceremony, when he went to the suppliant's lodge, where, after purifying the interior with incense, he prepared a canopy of buffalo-robes in the honor place. Beneath it he laid a robe upon which was placed a bowl-case—a basket of osiers and box-elder bark—the symbol of Old Woman Who Never Dies. A woman's dress of mountain-sheep skin was placed over the case, and was partially covered with a newly tanned elk-hide, soft and white. On top of this was a war-bonnet of eagle-feathers dyed red, and at each side were placed presents of robes and clothing. In front hung several buffalo-paunches on cottonwood stakes.

To the right of this altar a bed of sage was laid for the sacred vessel, which was completely enclosed in the inner skin of a buffalo-paunch stretched tight over the top, so as to form a drum. Small bunches of sage were inserted under the sinews that bound the skin. The drumsticks were about two feet long, with one end bent into a circle. The vessel thus prepared was symbolic of [the attendant spirits].

49 *The Sun Dancer* virtually dances on the spot for hours as preparation for self-punishment for 'strength and visions' in this major Plains' ceremony

Toward evening the people assembled, and, with the keeper of a sacred pipe in advance bearing this talisman, marched four times around the village, singing, 'The rain is coming, it is here.' They entered the lodge of the suppliant, and while the Keeper of the Bowl burned incense of sage, sweet-grass, and fir needles, the pipe-bearer laid the sacred pipe before the altar. The singers, eight or nine in number, gathered about the bowl, the medicine-men sitting at their right, and those who had come to fast ranging themselves to the left of the altar, each laying down an armful of sage, which was to serve as his bed during the four days and four nights of fasting.

The ceremonial dress was a buffalo-robe worn hairy side out-ward, and the participants painted themselves blue with clay from which pottery is made.

When all had entered, the singers chanted a wordless song, the burden of which was that the mystery-power had come. They stood up imitating the various birds that belong to the bowl,—ducks, geese, brant, and smaller birds,—while the fasters, rising, wailed to [the attendant spirits], as though they were lost children crying for their parents. Several other prayer-songs, without words, were sung, after which the Keeper of the Bowl sang 'Hi-hi-wa-hi,' signifying that the spirits had come. The singers swayed from side to side, and at the end of the song settled down, mimicking the actions of water-fowl and giving their cries.

The Keeper of the Bowl burned incense, and, taking some of the food previously brought in by relatives of the fasters, held it to the Four Winds and then offered it to Old Woman Who Never Dies with the prayer:

'Old Woman Who Never Dies, your mystery-powers are good. Now eat. Our young men have provided this food, that you may make them strong.'

The fasters now divided the food, and each of them took a bowl of it to one of the medicine-men, a clansman of his father. When the latter had finished eating, the faster placed his hands on the medicine-man's shoulders and stroked his arm to the wrists, as though receiving some power or virtue from him. His relative then sang to the spirits, imploring them to aid the faster.

The fasters next carried food to the spectators and the medicine-men, while the suppliant provided for the singers and the Keeper of the Bowl. Before eating, each one offered the food to the Four Winds and the altar. After the others had eaten and smoked, the suppliant and such of the fasters as chose came to the Keeper of the Bowl and the singers and were pierced as in the [Sun Dance]. Slits were cut in the flesh of each breast and the inserted rawhide ropes were fastened to the cross-timbers of the supporting posts of the lodge.

The devotees in a frenzied dance made violent efforts to free themselves. Buffalo-skulls were sometimes hung by thongs

passed through slits in the thighs or shoulders, and other fasters were pierced through the flesh of the shoulders and suspended, their feet clear of the ground.

The singers encouraged the dancers and kept their spirits at the highest pitch by wild singing and drumming. The fasters endured the torture as long as they were able; if they failed to tear themselves loose, or fainted with the intense pain, the Keeper of the Bowl and the singers cut the thongs and laid the exhausted dancers on their beds of sage, where they remained until the end of the ceremony, fasting and praying for visions.

While women were not permitted inside the lodge during the ceremony, some of them came and slept in the outer entrance, hoping to have dreams that might be favorably interpreted. They departed at the first sign of dawn, that their presence might not be discovered.

IV(1909), 156–158

Tricks Performed by Arikara Medicine Fraternities

The ceremony, [appropriately named Magic Performance,] began at the time of the ripening of squashes and continued until autumn, [and] consisted largely of legerdemain .... Each order of medicine-men had its appropriate songs and feats of magic, and each night was devoted to the performance of a single trick or set of tricks.

Following is a brief description of tricks from the repertoire of [some of the] orders:

The leader of the Ghosts, rising, held a human skull above his head and apparently swallowed it. Then while he lay flat on the floor, face downward, another Ghost covered him with a robe, and when the leader arose the skull was seen lying on the ground.

The Black-tail Deer stood forth in a row and sang; then one of them ran quickly outside, mounted to the roof, and whistled. In the distance was heard the answer of an elk, which was called closer and closer by the continued whistling of the medicine-man.

A skull of their animal was placed by the Buffalo men beside the southwestern centre-post, then all of them danced on the opposite side of the fire. Soon the skull appeared to bellow.

The Big Feet, wearing necklaces of duck-bills strung on otter-skin, ran to the waterside and brought back rushes, which a woman was engaged to set in the earth near the fireplace, typifying the marsh where ducks nest. Another woman was called upon, and to her they gave their necklaces, which she raised aloft to the north and then cast among the rushes. Straightway was heard a sound supposed to be the quacking of the spirit duck that was believed to dwell in the body of the leader. As the fire died down he passed to the opposite side of the fireplace and imitated the actions of a duck, and there was heard the sound of a large flock quacking, and flapping their wings in the water.

The Moon medicine-men spread a robe beside the fire, which

was then permitted to die down. The leader raised the robe and swung it several times through the air, and then a light was seen streaming down through the smoke-hole, yellow like the rays of the moon. A more spectacular trick was that performed by the same order, when they began by spreading a mat of dry rushes on the ground. The leader painted a black circle around his face, others about wrists and ankles, and a black spot on his chest. Sticks were set up and the rush mat was thrown over them, forming a miniature lodge. With a whistle and a small drum the medicine-man crawled under, and when he had disappeared the firekeeper ignited the mat, which blazed fiercely. Everybody shouted in excitement. When the little lodge was burned to the ground, no trace of the man was to be seen; but some of the people, going to the river, would see him emerging from the water, beating his drum, and staggering as if exhausted. Supported by brother medicine-men he entered the lodge and sat beside the fire, saying, 'I have travelled far. I have learned that we are going to have good crops and many buffalo.'

A round stone painted red lay back of the Mother Night medicine-men, who wore red paint on their legs, black on their bodies, and red spots over the black on their faces. The wife of a younger member came forward; her hair was then loosened and brushed, and her face painted. She touched the stone, then all the members of the order rolled it into the fireplace, while the keeper was told to build a great fire. When the stone was supposedly red-hot, the young assistant, who had been rubbed with medicine by the leader and encouraged to fear nothing, leaped upon it and 'danced,'—in reality he touched his feet to the stone a very few times,—supporting himself by a stout staff in each hand, while the flames singed his eyebrows and skin. Quickly he leaped through the flames to the opposite side, where the leader rubbed him with an infusion of herbs.

Connected with the medicine fraternity were several supernumeraries chosen by the members to perform the necessary manual labor. After a term as attendant a man had the privilege of buying the medicine of any order and thus becoming a member. Wishing to join the organization, a man first offered a pipe of tobacco to the cedar, crying the while, then he entered the lodge and extended the pipe first to the firekeeper, then to each group in order, beginning with the Ghosts. Finally making his way to the group he wished to join, he held out the pipe to their leader, but the medicine-man clenched his hands as if unwilling to accept it. The aspirant, however, forced them open and thrust the pipe into them, an act taken as a sign that he was to be initiated.

The pipe was then smoked in turn by all the medicine-men in the lodge. The novitiate stripped and was painted, not carefully on this first day, but rather hurriedly, and the painter received his clothing in payment. Medicine was rubbed over his body, and he drank a decoction of roots. From the hour of joining he assisted in the singing, learning thus the numerous songs of his medicine, and he was given some small part in the performance of tricks. He was, in fact, now servant to the selected group instead of to the entire fraternity. From time to time he was given further instruction in the mysteries of his medicine, and for each new lesson a fee was levied. Instruction was apparently not given willingly: there was no desire to help the novitiate become an adept at once. The initiation rather was in the nature of a contest between the older members and the younger, the latter striving to be taught immediately, the former bargaining for the amount of the payment, reserving their secrets and parting with them only after much persuasion and many promises.

When the leader of a group of the medicine fraternity died, the one who had learned the most from him became his successor. The number of members for each group was not fixed. It seems to have been usually four to six, though it must have been considerably larger in the days when the Arikara prospered.

V(1909), 65–70

Navaho: The Night Chant

A description of the ritual and form of the Yebichai ceremony, —Kleje Hatal, or Night Chant,—covering its nine days of performance, will give a comprehensive idea of all Navaho nine-day ceremonies, which combine both religious and medical observances. The myth characters personated in this rite are termed Yebichai, Grandfather or Paternal Gods. Similar personations appear in other ceremonies, but they figure less prominently.

First Day: The ceremonial, or medicine, hogan is built some days in advance of the rite. The first day's ceremony is brief, with few participants. Well after dark the singer, assisted by two men, makes nine little splint hoops— . . . *kedan*—entwined with slip-cords, and places them on the sacred meal in the meal basket. Following this, three men remove their everyday clothing, take Yebichai masks, and leave the hogan. These three masked figures are to represent the gods Haschelti, Talking God, Haschebaad, Goddess, and Haschelapai, Gray God. When they have gone and passed to the rear of the hogan, the patient comes in, disrobes at the left of the centre, passes around the small fire burning near the entrance of the hogan, and takes his seat in the centre, immediately after which the singing begins. During the third song Haschelti enters with his cross-sticks—*Haschelti balil*— and opens and places them over the patient's body, forcing them down as far toward the ground as possible. The second time he places them not so far over the body; the third, not lower than the shoulders; the fourth time, over the head only, each time giving his peculiar call, *Wu-hu-hu-hu-u*! Then Haschelti takes up a shell with medicine and with it touches the patient's feet,

50 *The Altar Complete*, a stage in the Foster Parent Cry, one of the major religious ceremonies of the Sioux

hands, chest, back, right shoulder, left shoulder, and top of head, —this being the prescribed ceremonial order,—uttering his cry at each placing of the medicine. He next places the shell of medicine to the patient's lips four times and goes out, after which Haschebaad comes in, takes one of the circle *kedan*, touches the patient's body in the same ceremonial order, and finally the lips, at the same time giving the slip-cord a quick pull. Next comes Haschelapai, who performs the same incantations with the *kedan*. Again Haschelti enters with the cross-sticks, repeating the former order, after which he gives the patient four swallows of medicine, —a potion different from that first given,—the medicine-man himself drinking what remains in the shell. This closes the ceremony of the first day. There will, perhaps, be considerable dancing outside the hogan, but that is merely practice for the public dance to be given on the ninth night. The singer and the patient sleep in the hogan each night until the nine days are passed, keeping the masks and medicine paraphernalia between them when they sleep.

Second Day: Just at sunrise the patient is given the first ceremonial sweat. This is probably given more as a spiritual purification than in anticipation of any physical benefit. To the east of the hogan a shallow hole is dug in the earth, in which are placed hot embers and ashes—covered with brush and weeds, and sprinkled with water—upon which the patient takes his place. He is then well covered with blankets. The medicine-man, assisted by Haschelti and Haschebaad, places about the patient a row of feathered *kedan*, and then commences to sing while the patient squirms on the hot, steaming bed. After singing certain songs the medicine-man lifts the blanket a little and gives the patient a drink of medicine from a ceremonial basket. He is again covered, and the singing goes on for a like time. Later the blankets are removed and Haschelti and Haschebaad perform over the patient, after which he goes to the hogan. The brush and weeds used for the bed are taken away and earth is scattered over the coals. This sweating, begun on the second day, is repeated each morning for four days: the first, as above noted, taking place west of the hogan, and the others respectively to the south, west, and north. The ceremonies of the second night are practically a repetition of those held the first night. During the third song Haschelti enters with the *Haschelti balil*, placing it four times in the prescribed order and giving his call; then he goes out, re-enters, and takes from the medicine basket four sacred reed *kedan*. These he carries in ceremonial order to the four cardinal points: first east, then south, next west, lastly north. Next stick *kedan* are taken out of the basket, which holds twelve each of the four sacred colors. These also are carried to the four cardinal points—white, east; blue, south; yellow, west; black, north. After all the *kedan* are taken out, Haschelti again enters with the *Haschelti balil*, using it in directional order and giving medicine as on the night before.

Third Day: It is understood that the patient has been sweated in the morning, as on the second day. On this night he is dressed in spruce boughs by the assisting medicine-man, bound around the wrists, arms, ankles, legs, and body, and fastened on the head in the form of a turban. After several songs, . . . the boughs [are cut] from the body, using a stone arrow-point as a knife. Then the boughs are cut into fragments over the patient's head, after which the singer takes a feather wand, points it toward the four cardinal points above the fire, and brushes the patient, chanting meanwhile. At the end of the brushing he points the wand out of the smoke-hole, at the same time blowing the dust from it out into the open air.

Fourth Day: The ceremonies this day do not begin until later than usual, probably nine o'clock. Haschelti and Haschebaad dress and go out. The patient disrobes and takes his place. The assisting medicine-man digs a small hole just between the patient's feet, and encircles it with a line of *taditin*, or pollen, leaving an opening to the east, after which the patient dons a mask. Haschelti enters, followed by Haschebaad, who carries a small spruce tree. The former puts sacred pollen in the hole four times, each time giving his call; then Haschebaad plants the tree in the hole and fastens its top to the patient's mask; the mask is then pulled off the patient's head by his jerking quickly away from the tree. This is the first night in which the ceremonies are continued until dawn. After the unmasking, the singers take their place at one side of the back of the hogan and begin singing to the accompaniment of a basket drum. A youth and a maiden are required to sit in the hogan throughout the fourth night, the ritual requiring that these be persons who have not had sexual knowledge.

Fifth Day: This is the last day of the sweating, and the day on which the first dry-painting is made. Just at dark this painting, a small one, is begun inside. In size it would square about four feet, and is placed close to the back of the hogan. There are three figures in the painting: the central one being the patient, the one to the left Haschelti, the one to the right Haschebakun, [a male deity]. Around this painting, at all sides except the eastern, feather wands . . . are stuck in the ground; in this case twelve in number. Foot-tracks are made in the sand with white meal. Haschelti and Haschebakun dress ceremonially, mask, and go out, after which the patient enters and takes his position on the central figure of the dry-painting, facing the east. The effort this night is to frighten the patient and thus banish the evil spirits from his body. The two maskers come running in, uttering weird, unearthly howls, in which every spectator in the hogan joins, feigning great fear. The masked figures make four entries, each like the other. In many cases the patient either actually faints from fright or feigns to do so. The patient then leaves the dry-painting and it is destroyed. None of the sand or other pigments used in this painting is applied to the patient's body, as is done with that of later paintings. The next part of the fifth night's ceremony is the initiation of new members into the Yebichai order. No one who is not a member of the order is allowed to enter the ceremonial hogan. At the time of the initiation Haschelti and Haschebakun are outside in the darkness. The initiates enter and sit on the ground in a row—the males naked, the women dressed in their ordinary mode. They dare not look up, for should they see Haschelti before being initiated, they would become blind. One at a time these novices take their place in the centre of the hogan and the initiatory rite is performed over them.

Sixth Day: This is the first day of the large dry-paintings. The painting is commenced early in the morning, and is not finished until mid-afternoon. The one on this day is the whirling log representation. After it is finished, feathers are stuck in the ground around it, and sacred meal is scattered on parts by some of the assisting singers. Others scatter the meal promiscuously; one of the maskers uses a spruce twig and medicine shell, applying meal to every figure and object in the painting. Then the medicine-men all gather up portions of the sacred meal, putting it in their medicine pouches. The patient soon enters and takes his seat in the centre of the painting. The usual incantations are gone through, after which the colored sands of the painting are applied to the corresponding parts of the patient's body, then gathered up and carried off to the north. During the day two sets of beggars go out to the neighboring hogans. These personate

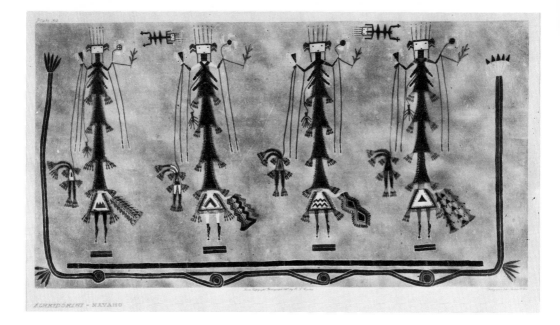

51 *Alhkidokihi*, one of the four dry paintings executed during the nine-day Navaho Mountain Chant

Haschelti, Tonenili—Water Sprinkler, the God of Water, who is really a clown—and as many Haschebaad as care to go out. The beggars carry whips made of yucca leaves, and one who does not respond to their appeals for gifts is whipped,—if he can be caught,—which creates a great deal of amusement. The personators act like a company of clowns, but at the same time they gather a large quantity of food. When the day is thoroughly taken up with dry-painting and ceremonies, there is less of the ceremonial at night. The medicine-men, to the accompaniment of the basket drum, sing for a short time only on this sixth night, while outside the late evening is spent in dancing by those who are later to participate in the closing dance.

Seventh Day: This day is practically consumed with the making of another large dry-painting. The masked men go out on another begging tour, also, and the medicine ceremonies and the destroying of the dry-painting are practically the same as those of the day before, while during the evening the medicine-men sing to the accompaniment of the drum.

Eighth Day: The dry-painting is finished about three o'clock in the afternoon. After its completion there is a large open-air initiation. To become a full member of the Yebichai order one must first be initiated in the hogan; the second initiation is a public one; the third, another inside the hogan; the fourth, another in the open. These different initiation ceremonies, the same in point of ritualism, may be carried over several years.

Ninth and Final Day: To the average person and to the Indians as a whole the last day is the Yebichai dance. From a distance the

Indians have been gathering during the two previous days, and the hospitality of the patient's family, as well as that of all the people living in the neighboring hogans, is taxed to the utmost. And from early morning until dark the whole plain is dotted with horsemen coming singly and in groups. Great crowds gather at the contests given half a mile from the hogan, where horse-races, foot-races, groups of gamblers, and throngs of Indians riding wildly from race-track to hogan fill the day with hilarity and incidents memorable to all. Toward the end of the day preparation is made for the closing part of the nine-day rite. Great quantities of fuel have been brought from the distant plateau, and placed in many small piles at each side of the smooth dance ground to the east of the hogan. As soon as it is dark the fuel is ignited, making two long lines of camp-fires, furnishing both light to see the dancers and warmth to the spectators, for the Yebichai cannot be held until the autumn frosts begin, when the nights have the sharp, keen air of the high altitudes.

With the gathering darkness the human tide flows toward the medicine hogan, illuminated in the dusk by the long lines of camp-fires. All gather about and close around the dance square, having to be kept back by those in charge. Men, women, and children sit on the ground near the fires. Many on horseback have ridden up, and form a veritable phalanx back of the sitting spectators. The dance does not begin at once, and those assembled spend the time telling stories, jesting, and gossiping. Belated arrivals make coffee, or do hurried cooking around the fires.

Some distance to the east of the dance ground is a brush enclosure where the dancers prepare for their part in the rite. There, too, is a fire for light and warmth. The men in preparation remove all clothing, save short kilts, and paint their bodies with a mixture of water and white clay. Anyone who may have ex- perienced the enjoyment of a sponge bath out in the open on a cold, windy night can appreciate the pleasure of the dance preparation. The dancers are impersonators of Navaho myth characters, twelve usually taking part. No qualifications are necessary other than that the participant be conversant with the intricate ritual of the dance. The dance continues throughout the entire night, one group of men being followed by another. The first twelve men dance through four songs, retiring to the dressing enclosure for a very brief rest after each. Then they withdraw, and twelve others dance for a like period, and so on. The first group sometimes returns again later, and the different groups vie with one another in their efforts to give the most beautiful dance in harmony of movement and song, but there is no change in the step. The several sets have doubtless trained for weeks, and the most graceful take great pride in being pro- nounced the best dancers. The first group of grotesquely masked men is ready by nine or ten o'clock; they file into the dance enclosure led by Haschelti, their naked, clay-painted bodies glinting in the firelight. While wearing masks the performers never speak in words; they only sing or chant. To address one in conversation would incur the displeasure of the gods and invite disaster. Time is kept by the basket drum and the rhythm of the singing.

The white visitor will get his best impression of the dance from a short distance, and, if possible, a slight elevation. There he is in touch with the stillness of the night under the starry sky, and sees before him, in this little spot lighted out of the limitless desert, this strange ceremonial of supplication and thanksgiving showing slight, if any, change from the same performance, held on perhaps the same spot by the ancestors of these people ages ago. As the night wears on the best group of dancers come out. They are, perhaps, from the Redrock country, or from some other far-away district, and have been practising for weeks, that they might excel in this dance. The most revered song of the Yebichai is the Bluebird song, which is sung at the approach of day, and is the closing act of the drama. With the last words, 'Dola anyi, dola anyi,' the assembled multitude start for their homes, near and far, melting into the gray of the desert morn, and by the time the sun breaks above the horizon the spot which was alive with people a few hours before is wrapped in death-like stillness, 1(1907), 116–124 not a soul being within range of the eye.

8 Arts and Crafts

Navaho Material Culture

While the Navaho leads a wandering life, the zone of his movements is surprisingly limited; indeed the average Navaho's personal knowledge of his country is confined to a radius of not more than fifty miles. The family usually has three homes, the situation of which is determined by the necessities of life. Near their summer home they cultivate small crops of corn and vegetables in narrow, sandy washes, where by deep planting sufficient moisture is insured to mature the crop. In a few sections small farming is conducted by means of irrigation. In Cañon de Chelly, which may be termed the garden spot of the reservation, there are diminutive farms and splendid peach orchards irrigated with freshet water.

Owing to its lowness and its earth covering, the Navaho house, or *hogan* is the most inconspicuous of habitations. One might ride from morning till night across the reservation and not observe either a hogan or an Indian, although he has no doubt passed within a stone's throw of many of these houses and been peered at by many more dark eyes from brush concealments. At the end of a long day in the saddle the traveller may wonder where the many thousands of Navaho reside; but his inquiry may be answered if he will but climb to the summit of one of the many low mountains and view the panorama as the long shadows of evening are creeping on. Here and there in every direction the thin blue smoke of the campfire may be seen curling upward as these desert people prepare their evening meal. In this clear, rare atmosphere the far distant horizon is the only limit to his vision. Just below, a mile or so away, may perhaps be seen the smoke from a group of half a dozen hogans. Miles beyond is another group, and still beyond another, and so throughout the sweep of vision.

The handicraft of the Navaho is seen at its best in their blanketry, which is one of the most important industries of any Indians within our domain. The greater portion of the wool from their hundreds of thousands of sheep is used in weaving, and in addition a considerable quantity of commercial yarn is employed for the same purpose. The origin of the textile art

among the Navaho is an open question. It is probable that they did not learn it from anyone, but that it developed as a part of their domestic culture. It is contended by some that the early Spanish missionaries taught the Navaho to weave; but why should the white man be accredited with this art? The mummies found in the prehistoric cliff-ruins of the Navaho country are wrapped in cloth finer than any ever produced with a Navaho loom, and no doubt now remains that Pueblo people were incorporated by the Navaho in ancient times.

The blankets made in earlier days, say from fifty to a hundred and fifty years ago, are beautiful examples of primitive handicraft. The body of a so-called bayeta blanket was woven of close-spun native wool, dyed dark blue, while the red pattern was from the ravellings of Spanish bayeta. Much of the beauty of the old blankets is due to the mellowing of the native colors by age, but practically none of these rare examples are to be found among the Navaho at the present time. The blankets of to-day may be roughly divided into three classes: 1. Those made from the close-spun native yarn dyed in the old colors and woven in the simple old patterns; when aged they closely resemble the old bayeta blankets. 2. Blankets woven in a great variety of designs from coarse, loose-spun yarn dyed with commercial dyes of many shades; these are the Navaho blankets of commerce. 3. Those woven from commercial or 'Germantown' yarn; they are of fine texture and sometimes beautiful, but lack interest in that their material is not of Indian production. Fortunately the decrease in the demand for blankets woven of commercial yarn is discouraging their manufacture.

The Navaho woman weaves her blanket not so much for profit as for love of the work. It is her recreation, her means of expressing imagination and her skill in execution.

Because of their pastoral life the Navaho are not villagers.

Their dome-shaped, earth-covered hogans are usually grouped two or three in the same locality. The summer house is a rude brush shelter, usually made with four corner posts, a flat top of brush, and a windbreak of the same material as a protection against the hot desert siroccos. The hogan proper, used for storage during the summer, affords a warm and comfortable shelter to its occupants through the cold winters of their high altitude. When a hogan is built it is ceremonially consecrated, and if an occupant should die in it, it is forever deserted and is called ... 'evil house.' No Navaho will go near such a house or touch anything taken from it. If a meal were cooked with decayed wood from a hogan a hundred years deserted, a Navaho, even if starving, could not be induced to partake of it.

The domestic equipment of the Navaho is simplicity itself and reflects the simple life of the tribe. Of household furniture there is none. The bedding consists usually of a few sheepskins; cooking utensils are earthen pots of their own making, and cups, knives,

53 An aged Hopi woman potter, absorbed in her work, mixes clay

and spoons of civilization. Plates they do not need, as the family eat directly from the pot in which the food is cooked. The principal food is mutton, boiled, and corn prepared in many ways. Considerable flour obtained from traders is consumed; this is leavened slightly and made into small cakes, which are cooked over the embers like Mexican tortillas.

Many of the Navaho men are skilled silversmiths. Every well-to-do Navaho possesses a silver belt consisting of a dozen or more wrought oval discs, each about two by three inches, fastened to a leather strap. Such a belt, weighing several pounds, is of course a valuable piece of property. The wearer may also have a broad silver bracelet set with turquoise, a heavy string of silver beads with a massive pendant of the same material, and a pair of deerskin leggings with a row of silver buttons on the outer side. Frequently their horses are gaily bedecked with bridles and saddles heavily weighted with silver ornaments. The long strap over the shoulder, from which the pouch of the medicine-man is suspended, is always studded with silver buttons. Mexican coins, especially the peso, are the principal source of all this silver-work, the Navaho preferring this coin to our own dollar because it is heavier. Buttons and beads also are made from American dimes and twenty-five cent pieces; the small beads from dimes, and the large ones from two coins of the same value. They learned silversmithing from the Mexicans, but since their first lessons have developed a high degree of individuality in the art. While the metal-work of the Navaho at the present time is practically all in silver, only a few copper objects being made, their earliest work in metal was with iron, and occasionally an example of this is found. The silver and shell bead jewelry of the Navaho is his savings bank. During times of prosperity he becomes the possessor of all the jewelry his means afford, and when poor crops or long winters threaten distress he pawns it at a trader's, so that many of the traders often have thousands of dollars' worth of silverwork and shell beads on hand at one time. The system seems to be a very fair one, and in times of stress is certainly a boon to the impecunious Navaho.

Most Navaho ceremonies are conducted, at least primarily, for the purpose of healing disease: and while designated medicine ceremonies, they are, in fact, ritualistic prayers . . . . Each is based on a mythic story, and each has four dry-paintings, or so-called altars. Besides [the] nine days' ceremonies there are others whose performance requires four days, and many simpler ones requiring only a single day, each with its own dry-painting.

The figures shown in the dry-paintings are conventionalized representations of the characters in Navaho mythology and of incidents in the myth. With how many such paintings the Navaho medicine-men are familiar is an unanswered question; but more than sixty have been noted, some of them most elaborate. In making them, the ground within the ceremonial hogan is evenly covered with fine brown earth, upon which the figures are drawn with fine sands and earths of many colors allowed to flow between the thumb and the first two fingers. The Navaho become so skilled in this work that they can draw a line as fine as a broad pencil mark. Many of the paintings are comparatively small, perhaps not more than four feet in diameter; others are as large as the hogan permits, sometimes twenty-four feet across. To make such a large painting requires the assistance of all the men who can conveniently work at it from early morning until mid-afternoon.

I(1907), 73–78

The Painting of Tipis by the Sarsi

Tipis symbolically painted in a manner prescribed in a dream are held in high regard, because no ill luck comes to those who live in them and because they bring a good price when transferred. Each painted tipi has an individual name referring to its decoration and to the 'flag' hanging from its peak. A native readily identifies such a tipi by its name.

The following narrations are typical of the dream experiences in which painted tipis are acquired.

North of Calgary is an elevation called Nose hill. Near by are several lakes called Rolling lakes from the rough, rocky character of the country. It was winter. I was a grown man, sliding down [that is, past twenty-five, at which age a man gave up participation in youthful amusements]. I was on the hill looking around and saw my father come out of his tipi with a gun on his shoulder. I went down to my grandfather's and changed my moccasins. I dressed well and took my knife. I followed my father's tracks. I went some little distance, and then heard the gun. A little farther I came upon buffalo-tracks. I saw drops of blood and followed them up to a slough, and there I saw a buffalo on its back. I did not see my father. I began to butcher it. The head was pointing east. I cut a piece of fat from the breast, sat down on the head, and started to eat. I heard another shot. It was growing late. I heard a wind coming, and soon it began to snow hard. I lay down in the shelter of the buffalo. It became dark. All night it snowed. My father did not know I had followed him. In the middle of the night I lost my senses. The buffalo spoke: 'My son, I have pity for you. I will give you my tipi. You see this gray hair on my head? I will give you that also. Here is my tail; I give you that. Now see the tipi I give you.' The tipi faced eastward. There was a buffalo painted on the left and one on the right. 'My son, do not fear to make this tipi. I am the one who with six others came out of the mountains. Pray to me; I am jealous; do not pray to any other.' The tipi had a calf-skin hanging

54 *Painted Tipi—Assiniboin*

from its peak. I looked at the tipi again, and it was covered with buffalo. 'Do not give this tipi away to other tribes. Keep it among your own people. All evil will fail to touch you so long as you live in this tipi.' That is how I got a painted tipi. I made one just like that when the time came, a few years ago. I have now had it nearly four years, and when the fourth year has passed I shall have to transfer it to someone. The Buffalo gave me four songs to go with the tipi.

About thirty years ago I lost a horse that I was keeping for old times' sake. I thought he was mired somewhere, so I went down along the creek looking for him. I followed the creek and saw a beaver-dam. A man stood there. I came up to him. He told me to wait. Then I lost myself. I heard someone singing in the beaver-dam. There were two songs. An old man with matted hair came out, followed by a woman. The man had a digging-stick wrapped in a skin, and the woman had a bundle. A girl came behind them and had a beaver-skin draped over her right shoulder. They went around the way the sun goes. The man stood next to me, then the woman, then the girl, on the north side of me. He said: 'My son, look toward that slough. We are going into the tipi. This tipi I will give you.' He took me into his tipi under the dam. The woman laid the bundle at the back opposite the door. 'Four days I will mark for you. What has happened here you must not reveal during these four days.' He gave me two songs. Two days passed and this woman of mine asked me, 'Why are you so without life?' I told her what had happened to me. Then I was sorry I had told her. I went back to the dam. The man appeared to me again. He said: 'I will give you only this tipi which you saw, and nothing else. I was going to give you something more, but you have not listened to me. My name is Chief Beaver. I have another house on Bow river.' I got nothing except the tipi. It was all yellow and had a dark beaver on each side at the back, and another pair on the sides near the door . . . I have not yet made this tipi. Some time I will paint it.

XVIII(1928), 114–116

Yokuts Basketry

Basketry was formerly the principal, as it remains the only, manufacturing industry, and here the Yokuts exhibit more skill and artistry than in any other field. Both the coiled and the twined processes are followed.

The materials for coiled basketry are the stems of a grass which the Chukchansi call *chinis* (Xerophyllum?) for the multiple foundation, and shreds of the root-stock of a sedge, *solosul*, for the wrap. Black designs are effected by an overlay wrapping of root fibres of *sapasip* (dwarf fir?) dyed by burial in mud; and reddish designs by the use of the bark of redbud, *monohil*. A recent innovation is to add bits of a brighter ornamentation by employing the orange-colored quills of the yellowhammer.

Among the examples of coiled work are cooking baskets, which have flat bottoms, slightly flaring sides, and maximum diameter at the upper edge, where they are from eighteen to twenty-four inches wide; globose baskets, large and small, with restricted openings, for containing trinkets and other small objects; approximately hemispherical food baskets, sixteen to twenty inches broad, into which cooked mush is poured and from which the entire family eats, each one dipping in the tips of his bunched fingers and rapidly conveying to his mouth that which adheres; and finally, shallow, tray-like parching baskets.

Materials for twined work include *Rhus trilobata* and redbud rods for both warp and weft, fir-root for weft, and redbud-bark and dyed fir-roots for overlaid weft to produce designs of red and black respectively. These materials are used in various combinations. The cradle-basket, which consists of a base and a separate shade lashed to it, the conical burden-basket, and the utility basket with opening slightly smaller than the base and used for storage of basketry materials and other objects, are made of *Rhus trilobata* warp and weft, with overlay of redbud-bark and blackened fir-root. *Rhus trilobata* warp, fir-root weft, and redbud-bark ornamentation appear in the shovel-shape, or some-

what triangular, sifters and the shallow bowls called 'tortilla containers.' A scoop-shape, open-mesh utensil with the warp-rods all converging into a handle, is made of redbud rods for warp and weft, some with the bark removed, others with the reddish bark intact. The seed-beater, of the same general shape and construction, has *Rhus trilobata* warp and redbud weft.

In the southern part of Yokuts territory, especially in the lake district, willow is much used in basketry; but in former times when the country was covered with tules, and willow and other basketry materials were not at hand, baskets of various types, including water containers, were made of tules. It is said that the water vessels were not gummed, and the swelling of the strands when wet made them fairly water-tight. Tule balsas were the work of a few men who specialized in this industry, but in all the valley country tule mats were made in quantity, to serve as house-walls, mattresses, and cushions. It is possible that the adoption of the potter's art among the southern Yokuts was due largely to the scarcity of suitable materials for basketry.

XIV(1924), 155–156

Kutenai Canoes

Inhabiting a mountainous country dotted with lakes and traversed by long winding rivers, the Kutenai very naturally became expert boatmen. The commoner form of craft was a canoe made of pine-bark or spruce-bark laid over a framework of split fir. It was sharp at bow and stern, of the form still seen among the Kalispel. Another type consisted of a skeleton framework and a covering of fresh elk-hides sewn together and well stretched, which dried stiff and hard. This formed a remarkably seaworthy craft, very wide of beam and so bulging amidships as to be, in effect, rather more than half-decked. Both ends were noticeably rounded and upcurving, the canoe giving the impression of being closely patterned on the lines of a water-fowl. In the summer of 1909 a canvas-covered specimen of the rounded-end type was discovered on the shore of Flathead lake, and was used in making a number of Kutenai pictures. It was seventeen feet in length, forty-seven inches in extreme width, twenty-three inches in

56 *A Kutenai Camp* depicting the canoe mentioned here in 'Kutenai Canoes'

depth, forty-two inches in height at the bow and thirty-seven inches at the stern. The Kutenai made dugouts of cottonwood logs only after steel axes were acquired.

Alaskan Eskimo Kaiaks

The kaiak . . . is the most important craft of many of the Alaskan Eskimo, for by means of it the livelihood of the people is chiefly obtained. Men transport themselves from one hunting camp to another in the kaiak; from it they fish, spear waterfowl, and pursue seal and walrus. Almost as soon as a boy can walk, he learns to paddle and manœuvre this small but efficient craft.

New kaiaks are made in late winter or in early spring during the season of . . . 'Mother of Rivers'—when rivers begin to open up. Their construction takes place with ceremony in the men's house, usually under the supervision of some old man well skilled in boat-making. The men measure and cut each individual part of the wooden frame according to a prescribed system based on the length of various members of the body or a combination of such members. Thus each man's kaiak is built according to the specifications of his own body and hence is peculiarly fitted to his use. For instance, the length of a kaiak is determined by the following standards of length: Little finger to elbow; first

57 Boys in Kaiak—Nunivak Eskimo

finger of right hand to thumb of left when arms are outstretched; elbow to middle finger; the span of middle finger to thumb; first finger of right hand to thumb of left when arms are outstretched; the width of first and second fingers held together. After each part is meticulously made according to measurement, the frame is put together with lashings of rawhide. The workmanship must of necessity be fine, because no cutting with edged tools may be done once the parts are finished and are being joined. The measurement of a typical Nunivak kaiak showed a length of fifteen feet over all, a beam of three feet, and a manhole thirty inches in diameter.

The kaiak frame consists first of a keel with bow and stern posts. The curved ribs, lashed to the keel, are mortised into the gunwales. A number of longitudinal strips extend from bow to stern, and the ribs are lashed also to these. The deck is formed by many slightly triangular supports or crossbeams whose ends are mortised and lashed into the gunwales. Two strips, one from bow to manhole and one from stern to manhole, run along the apexes of the deck supports and form ridge-poles. Slightly abaft the centre is the manhole, framed with a wooden hoop about thirty inches in diameter, lashed to the framework of the kaiak. The bow for hunters and married men may have a hole some three inches in diameter, used mainly for mooring or towing. The stern for this type has a quadrate projection several inches long and either straight or slightly upturned.

The night after the lashing of the kaiak frames is completed, the women gather to cut sealskins to size for the coverings, three thick and heavy hair-seal skins for the bottoms and sides, and two spotted-seal skins for the lighter decking. As they work, the women wear waterproof parkas, which are believed to prevent any evil influence from entering or afflicting the new kaiaks. After the cutting is finished, the women prepare food for the men.

The following day, while the women, dressed as before, are sewing together the skins, the kaiak owners sit before the bows of the completed frames and sing their hunting songs in an almost inaudible tone, since these songs are both sacred and secret. Kaiak owners often have their sons beside them to learn these chants, which descend from father to son. After the singing, when the hides are nearly sewn, each wife brings to her husband a new wooden dish of fish or berries. Stripped to the waist, he throws a portion of the food to the floor as an offering, and prays for good luck during the coming hunting season. He then gives the food to the oldest man present (often the one who has supervised the kaiak-making), who distributes it to all the men at hand. The owner then walks once about the kaiak frame, pretending to carry a lighted lamp. Next he motions as if to shove a lamp underneath the bows, that seal may see and approach his kaiak as he hunts.

As the last flap, on the after-deck, is sewn, after the frame is shoved into the completed covering, the now naked owner, accompanied by all the men present, sings his childbirth song to his new kaiak. The owner washes the cover with urine to remove any oil that may adhere to the surface, and rinses it in salt water. He then hauls his craft through the smoke-hole of the house and rests it in the snow, which will absorb dampness from its surface. Later he puts the kaiak on its rack and drapes over it his talismans, strung on belts, which [will] be kept in the kaiak. Here it remains a day and a night. Then at night he carries the craft to the ice where he sings his hunting songs, sacred only to him and to his family. Outside in the freezing weather the skin coverings bleach white. As soon as each new kaiak is finished, the owner performs his ceremony.

58 *Holiday Trappings—Cayuse*

On returning to the men's house, the owner dresses in new parka and boots, and, grasping a bunch of long grass fibres, makes motions of sweeping toward the entrance. By this action he brushes outside any evil influence or contamination from his kaiak, the covering of which has been made by women.

The kaiaks for hunters and married men are painted and inscribed with the owner's talismanic mark in the spring hunting camp in the following season of . . . 'When young seals are born'. Boys, youths, and young unmarried men have no talismanic devices on their kaiaks.

Near the bow is drawn or painted the head of the bird, animal, or fish representing the spirit-power of the owner. A narrow line running from stem to stern symbolizes the body. This line terminates in animal, fish, or bird tails or flukes according to the nature of the drawing. Near bow and stern the fins, flippers, or legs are drawn and in each case the male genital organ is represented. One craft had a combination mark of fowl and mink; another bore a representation of both white and red fox .The former had legs and wings in the same body, and the latter had both animals drawn separately. The belief is that the spirit-power of the animal will become embodied in the kaiak and aid materially in catching game. The original talismans may be the shaved noses of land animals, such as bear, mink, or fox; or birds, or sea animals, and are often objects carved from ivory or wood. These are kept in a wrapping of bark inside of a parchment roll of hair-seal bladder and are taken from their coverings only during the Bladder feast, when they are worn on headgear. When a man dies, his talismans are all wound in one bundle and given to the surviving sons; or, failing sons, are divided amongst the nearest relatives. Usually some particular talisman is handed down in a family from father to son.

The possessor of a talisman acquires supernatural power through the spirit of the animal, bird, or fish which it represents. A man's mark on kaiak, masks, weapons, or walrus- and seal-skins, is a medium through which the spirit-power always keeps in touch with the owner. It is also a mark of identification. It is taboo for a man to eat, wear, or even touch the animal, bird, or fish which his talisman represents, for his spirit would then be destroyed.

The finished kaiak, with hooks and lashings properly adjusted and a paddle set upright to represent the owner, when drawn up on shore or placed on racks is pointed seaward so that the spirit-power of the kaiak may always be thinking of and watching out for game.

Nunivak kaiaks are broader of beam, deeper of draft, and heavier than those of the mainland farther north, which are very narrow of beam and light of draft. Those of King Island and south of the Yukon mouth, both north and south of Hooper bay, are similar to the craft of Nunivak. The open water, rarely smooth, necessitates a sturdy craft. Often killing and cutting up his game far from home, either on the water or the ice, the hunter must have room beneath the decking for loading meat, which the deep draft provides. Around home waters it is not uncommon to see two people riding a kaiak, one facing aft, the other paddling. These seemingly frail craft are in reality very seaworthy, riding rough waters safely. The lashed framework readily yields to wave action, while a rigidly constructed boat would pound, and the decking sheds sea and spray alike. Besides the occupant, a kaiak carries a full complement of weapons, food, tools, and paddles, and, if the hunt has been successful, a load of meat, fish, or birds. The kaiak is used also for cruising along the shore and gathering driftwood. If the weather becomes too stormy for safety, two boats are tied together with thongs carried for that purpose. To relieve the monotony of the sitting position, skilful paddlers sometimes propel the boat standing up. Adept men can upset a kaiak and right it again with a paddle.

The ordinary kaiak equipment, other than weapons, consists of two single-bladed paddles ..., one held in reserve in case of possible breakage or loss, and a small paddle ... for use in working a kaiak near a seal before the spear is cast. The small paddle, a sculling blade, is used on the side of the kaiak away from the seal; thus the kaiak, while ever moving closer, appears to be drifting, there being no perceptible movement to frighten the intended quarry.

The paddler has beneath him a seat ... of wooden slats to keep him dry from the inevitable seepage. For his further comfort a grass mat ... is provided to sit on or to be used as a windbreak or as a ground cloth for sleeping when out overnight on the ice.

[Other items of essential equipment for each kaiak are: a combination landing hook, boat hook and ice-pick; a smaller hook; a walrus skin water bag; an air-bag or float made from a whole baby seal skin; fishing lines; line tray; a sled; ivory ice knives; and eye shades or goggles to protect the eyes from the snow glare.]

XX(1930), 12–13, 15–17

Kwakiutl Theatrical Practices

The tohwit trick of removing the entrails consists in laying the intestines of a seal on the woman's abdomen and covering them with a piece of seal-skin colored to the light-brown tint of her body. The seal-skin is then cut and the seal's intestines are removed, and the uninitiated believe that they are beholding a miracle. Another trick is to have a red-hot stone placed on the head, which is protected by a circular piece of wood covered with well-soaked cedar-bark fibre, the whole being concealed by the tohwit head-band.

An informant once saw a tohwit of a visiting tribe begin to dance and utter her cries the moment the canoe grounded, indicating her desire to have her head struck with a stone hammer. So a hammer was produced, and the woman stood in the canoe. A man raised the stone and seemed to strike her on the forehead with all his strength, and there was heard a resounding thud caused by a simultaneous blow on a heavy timber. The woman fell overboard backward and lay face downward in the water, and she remained in that situation more than an hour. The informant afterward asked the chief of that tribe how it was done, and received the explanation that pieces of bladder-kelp had been joined into a long tube, one end of which was held in the woman's mouth while the other was concealed among the beach stones.

Other ingenious feats of the tohwit involve apparent decapitation, transfixing with a spear, splitting of the shoulder with a paddle, and driving a wedge into the temple.

[Further tohwit initiate tricks include the following: having] a wooden image of a man rise from the ground and an eagle [on wires] descend from the roof and carry it away. ... [A]nother is that in which a box stands behind the singers, just high enough to be seen by the spectators. Water is poured into it, the initiate makes gestures toward it, uttering her cries, and presently a wooden loon bobs to the surface. It dives, and reappears. This happens four times. Then the woman calls for an eagle-tail, and with it she makes motions over the box, when a cloud of eagle-down flies upward. This is managed by a man who, concealed behind the singers, controls the wooden loon with strings running through the bottom of the box. After the loon trick is performed, he draws a plug, and the water runs into a pit and sinks into the ground. Through a hole in the side of the box is inserted the neck of a seal-bladder filled with eagle-down. He presses the bladder between his knees and the feathers fly upward. The uninitiated believe that they issue from the water.

In 1846 at Kalokwis on Turnour island, ... there were two tohwit initiates at a dance given by Numuqis, chief of the gens Sintlum. After the bear dancers had performed, the two young women appeared. They kept making signs and sounds to the interpreter, signifying their wish to be burned, and a quantity of logs which were there in readiness was built up into a high, square crib in the middle of the house. Outside in secret two young female slaves had been bound on two long boards. They were told: 'All the time you are in the fire, you must say *we, we, we*! and we will bring you to life, if you keep this up. If you do not say *we, we, we*! and if you scream, you will remain dead!' While this was being done, the attendants in the house tied the two tohwit to boards in the same manner, and took them outside, ostensibly to carry them to the roof and thence lower them into

59 A 'begged from' cedar in Kwakiutl territory, a living tree from which a plank has been taken

the fire. But outside the door they were released and the two slaves were hauled to the roof, constantly uttering their cry. They were bound to the boards at full length, and they moved their hands upward with the characteristic motion of the tohwit. In this position they were pushed down through an opening in the roof until the ends of the boards rested inside the roaring crib of logs. The slaves continued to utter the cry of the tohwit until they were dead. There was not a scream, so great was their dependence on the promise that they would be brought to life. The boards burned in twain, and the remains disappeared among the blazing logs. [This may have been an even more ingenious trick than the informant said, one involving the substitution of stuffed figures for the slaves.]

After the fire was burned out, the attendants gathered up the charred bones and placed them in two boxes, which were set in the corner of the house. All the tohwit women gathered round them, singing their secret songs, and soon was heard the sound of faint singing inside the boxes and the two tohwit came out.

Many of the dancers practise these sleight-of-hand tricks, which pass for magic. . . . [F]or example, [one] may walk about the house making restless motions with his hands and uttering his cries. A noise of something dropping on the housetop is heard, then a wooden kingfisher appears under the roof, and while the dancer continues his mystic motions, the bird descends. Whatever way the man goes, the bird follows, and when it reaches his level it darts at him and seemingly thrusts its long bill through his wrist. He resumes his gestures, and the bird mounts and disappears through the roof. There is an accomplice on the roof to release and draw up the bird, but its movements are also controlled by the dancer himself, who while apparently making the gestures by which he exerts magic power is really winding or unwinding on his wrists a pair of strings, which lower or raise the bird. . . . Suddenly a big hand comes up from the ground behind the singers, and a great rattle descends from the roof. The hand grasps and shakes it, and the sound of the rattle is heard. The hand releases it, and both disappear. Strings managed from the roof control these movements. One raises the hand, another lowers the rattle; others close the fingers of the hand, and still another, passing through the handle of the rattle, lifts a weight which holds down the pebbles therein and prevents them from making a noise inopportunely.

X(1915), 210–214

9 Food, Hunting and Fishing

An Apsaroke Winter Hunt (as related by Hunts to Die)

That night, [around the year 1860,] the chief gave orders: 'In the morning camp must be broken early, and we will go to the creek beyond East Pryor creek.' This was a long journey, but we made it. During the night at Muddy creek everybody was grinding knives, sharpening arrow-points, and testing bow-strings, for the next day the hunters were to start out while the camp moved down East Pryor to Pryor creek. We were very anxious to kill buffalo, for though everybody had parfleches full of buffalo-berries and a little elk-meat, that did not taste good; too much elk-meat is not good.

Early in the morning, when the women began to throw down the lodges, we started, wearing flannel overcoats with hoods of buffalo-hair, and buffalo-skin mittens fastened to the shoulders with strings. Besides the coats we had buffalo-robes, for the weather was very cold. We crossed Pryor creek, and just then a hard cold wind fell on us and the fine snow was thrown in our faces. That was the coldest day I can remember. It was so cold that the order was given to run the buffalo, kill some, cut out a few pieces of meat, and then rush for camp. I rode a big bald-face horse, the fastest one in the party. My saddle was a little pad cinched around the horse, and it had stirrups. My father was with me; though he was an old man, he was strong, and I gave him my riding horse, saying, 'I will kill a fat buffalo, and you come to me quickly.' The cold went into the skin, and we could not even throw off our robes to shoot. When we got very close to the buffalo they began to run through the snow, but I was soon in the herd and alongside of one whose back was broad. My knees almost touched her, and I put an arrow into her side. Then before my hand was bad I sent another arrow into another fat one and jumped off my horse, and while he ran around me I put my hands under my arms. They were stiff and had no feeling.

My father rode up and cut the buffalo down the belly, took my hands and thrust them in between the two sides. It was just like putting them into fire; the ends of the fingers pricked as if cactus needles were going into them, and I wanted to pull my hands out but he held them there. When he took them out, the finger-nails were black. He rubbed my hands in the snow, then I put them under my arms again, and soon I was able to use them. In a short time we had the buffalo cut up and the pieces strung together as they should be; we threw them on the horses, hurried to the other buffalo and cut it open, took out the calf, and ran for the camp. Most of the men took only a few pieces. My father was riding the fast horse and I the packhorse, sitting on the load of meat; but it was too cold, so I jumped on and drove the horses before me on a run.

We found our lodges all pitched, and inside the fires were leaping and cracking. The moment the heat struck our bodies it made them tremble. Every man in the party had either hands or face cooked by cold, but that night we all feasted and were happy. The next morning the weather was better, and we took short-handled axes and cut up the meat that had been left on the ground, We stayed in that place for a long time, for buffalo kept coming in from different parts of the country for shelter along the creek.

IV(1909), 115–116

Piegan: Offering the White Buffalo Skin

The white buffalo, as with other tribes, was sacred, and to take one in the hunt was an important matter. However, its killing and dressing were not attended with the elaborate ceremony observed by the Sioux and some other tribes. If one was found in the herd, great effort was made by the hunters to kill it. When shot, they say, it fell with its head to the east, where the sun rises. Without dismounting, the hunter called for some other man in the party and said to him, 'I give you this white buffalo.' The other man pondered, and if he had in his herd an especially fine horse, he said to the one who killed the buffalo, 'I accept it.' Then the killer rode away and the other dismounted and set fire to some buffalo-chips, one of which he laid at the animal's nose, another at the tail, another at the feet, and a fourth at the back. Then on each burning chip he placed sage, and with a bunch of sage he wiped the blood from the animal's wounds. Next he carefully skinned it, removing every particle of skin from the face and even to the edge of the hoofs. Leaving the meat, he wrapped the skin in a robe, mounted his horse, and rode to his home. There he ordered his best horse to be brought and tied in front of his lodge. The skin he took into the lodge, where a space was cleared before the place of honor, and there he laid the bundle. He ordered food prepared, and called out an invitation to the man who had killed the buffalo. After the feast and the smoke, he said, 'There is your horse outside.' Then the skin was dressed, without formality, the head-skin and the tail remaining attached to the hide. The owner wore it on special occasions, and after keeping it for a year or two, he prepared a feast, laid the skin in the place of honor, put some presents beside it, sent for a good horse, and tied it in front of the lodge. Then he summoned a medicine-man who knew all the sweat-lodge songs. When the singer entered the lodge, the owner of the skin gave him the pipe, and said: 'That horse outside is yours. I wish you to sing the songs of the sweat-lodge, for I am going to give this skin to the Sun.' So the priest sang the first seven sweat-lodge songs, those given by the sun, and then began again to sing them, at the same time painting on the skin with black an arch for the course of the sun, a circle for the moon, another circle for the morning star, and at the sides of these, two straight lines for the sun-dogs. He finished the painting as the seventh song was reached for the second time, and instructed the owner of the skin to place it in a certain tree, if any trees were in that vicinity, or on a hill or a high rock. The owner obeyed, with many prayers to the sun for good luck. Occasionally such a robe was offered to the sun by placing it in the fork of the centre-pole of the medicine-lodge before it was raised.

VI(1911), 14–15

Some Salishan Hunting Practices

When the first snow fell, the autumn hunting began, practically every person in the tribe participating, and each family taking its rush lodge. A man whom some spirit had supposedly endowed with supernatural ability particularly applicable to hunting, who, furthermore, had revealed this fact at the winter ceremony and had later proved himself, was the director of the hunt. He always led the party of hunters, and when he reached the edge of the gully or basin which he proposed to beat, he halted, sat down, and smoked. Then he directed the men to surround the area and drive the game out of cover, while he himself walked through

60 This Cree hunter is imitating the call of a male moose to bring the female within shooting range

the middle. If his medicine was potent, the deer were found to be not wild: they stood and looked at the hunters. If the hunting continued to be unsuccessful for some days, the leader would say to the others: 'I have not dreamed of a deer. For many days we have hunted, and I have been lying awake, but I cannot dream of a deer. I am afraid. Perhaps some one of you has dreamed.' If in the party there was anybody who as a child had been promised by some spirit animal that he should always be a good hunter, he would come forth and say that he had had a dream. He would then relate it, and predict the killing of a certain kind of animal at a certain time of day. If the prediction proved correct, he became the leader of the hunt, and would sing his songs in the coming winter's ceremony. An old Spokan illustrated the part religious belief plays in hunting by the following narration:

> Before white men came, animals and people used to talk to each other. One year we were having very bad luck in the tribal hunt. Some days the whole party, which was a large one, killed one or two deer, never more. We were in the Okanagan country. I was feeling very sorry. One night, while I slept, Badger, who was my medicine, said to me: 'Look at that gully. I will appear on the other side in the form of a grizzly-bear. To-morrow go into that gully, and if you kill me you may as well turn back to your own country, for you will not kill any deer. If you do not kill me, you may stay here and hunt, and you will have good luck. When you reach that gully, do not put any one on the western side of it, but go on that side yourself. If you put any of your boys on the western side, I will kill one of them.' When, the next day, we arrived at the place Badger had shown me, the head-man told us which way to go. He sent my son and my grandson to the western side, one above and one below, and I went in the middle. I was anxious, wondering if the grizzly-bear would kill one of my boys. By and by I heard the bushes crack, and the noise of something coming. I thought it was one of my boys. Across the creek I waited on a rocky bench. I could hear my boy near by whistling. Then I heard the grizzly-bear coming behind me. He was following me. I went back a little way and saw him; I raised my gun and he still came on, so I shot, and he threw himself down, but quickly jumped up on a rock, where I shot him again. He then ran into the brush. My son came, and we chased him, but he got away.

VII(1911), 79–80

Rabbit Hunting by The Keres of Cochiti

Hunting was usually a communal undertaking, and the rabbit-drive may still be observed. In ordering a hunt the war-chiefs name the fourth day following, counting the day of announcement as the first, and say, 'All the game shall be given to . . . the cacique.' The hunt-chief, . . . 'cougar man', is the head of the Shayak, a society having ceremonial control of game and hunting.

Arriving at the place from which the hunt is to start, the Cougar Man builds a small fire in such a way that a thin column of smoke rises. This he keeps burning during the hunt, and from time to time he smokes cigarettes and prays for good luck to the hunters. He is attended by a youth who carries his quiver, his tobacco, and a cedar-bark fire-rope.

When all the men have assembled at the appointed place, two young men selected by the war-chiefs are sent by Cougar Man in opposite directions to encircle a large area and pass each other at a given point. Behind each of these two follow half of the hunters, each party in charge of several young men appointed by the war-chiefs and armed with bunches of willow switches. At regular intervals of perhaps a hundred yards these deputies designate a man to stop and stand guard, until the entire area is enclosed. Each hunter carries two rabbit-sticks, usually of oak, with a heavy knobbed end, one in the right hand, the other in the belt. In the left hand are the bow and half a dozen arrows. Some have quivers on the back.

When the leaders pass each other at the opposite side of the circle, they shout: . . . '[The circle is closed!]' This is repeated in turn by each man in the circle until the signal is received at the starting point, when all begin to converge slowly. If a rabbit escapes between two men, then when the hunt is ended they are denounced by their companions, and standing with arms outstretched, . . . they both are whipped at the same time.

When the hunters meet at the centre of the circle, they proceed to enclose another tract, and so continue through the day. They return to the village at sunset, but before they enter the war-chief calls, 'All you who have killed game, bring it here!' They pile their rabbits, hares, gophers, and birds before him, and he says, 'All this is for . . . the cacique, who is also called . . . all-our mother.' He orders his deputies to carry the game to the cacique and dismisses the hunters.

In the morning young men come to skin the game and hang it up to dry. It is given to the cacique, not for use in public feasts but for the subsistence of his household; for he is too important a personage and too busy with religious duties to hunt and farm. Whenever he needs meat a hunt of this kind is ordered. To supply themselves with meat the others hunt in smaller parties or by themselves. XVI(1926), 74-75

Some Kwakiutl Hunting Practices

It used to be the custom that when the first bear of the season was killed, the hunter would bring it to the village, and while yet a

61 *Fishing With a Gaff Hook—Paviotso*. He fishes in one of the saline inland seas, Walker Lake, Nevada

short distance away he would call, 'I have a visitor!' Then all the people very solemnly and quietly would assemble in his house. The bear was placed in a sitting posture in the place of honor at the middle of the back part of the room, with a ring of cedar-bark about its neck and eagle-down on its head. Food was then given to each person, and a portion was placed before the bear. Great solemnity prevailed. The bear was treated as the honored guest, and was so addressed in the speeches. The people, one by one, would advance and take its paws in their hands as if uttering a supplication. After the ceremonial meal was over, the bear was skinned and prepared for food.

On a certain night in the month of July when the tide will be at its lowest for that moon, spearsmen take their spears and watch throughout the night, waiting for a streak of light to shoot up from a star of the constellation 'spearsman of heaven' to one of the 'seven star' group. Then they hurl their spears at some object, in order to have good luck in their hunting. If a man finds himself threatened by drowsiness, he sets his wife to watch, and she arouses him when the flash comes.

X(1915), 38

Sarsi: The Hunting of Eagles

The capture of eagles involved long religious rites. When a man intended to hunt them, he and the occupants of four or five other tipis, those who desired to obtain feathers to be made into head-dresses, moved apart from the rest of the band and camped in the region of the proposed trap. During his hunt the people under-stood that if a bird perched on or near a tipi, they were not to name the bird but simply say, 'A young man is sitting on such and such a tipi.' To name the bird would have given the hunter bad luck. Rosehips were temporarily taboo, for they would have caused the eagles to scratch themselves and avoid the trap. Quiet in the camp was essential. Should a hunter, in spite of a violated taboo, try to catch eagles and fail, camp was struck immediately. The hunter practised continence, and ate and drank only before sunrise and after sunset. Eagle-hunters were middle-aged or elderly men of great patience.

On the top of a hill far from camp the eagle-hunter dug a hole extending east and west, and only a little larger than was necessary to admit him. He covered it with sticks and leaves, which were supported by three cross-pieces, and left a small aperture. The bottom he covered thickly with white sage. With rawhide he bound to a cross-piece of the roof the bait, a small animal, such as a wolf, with a piece of skin cut away from the ribs so as to expose the flesh. Before concealing himself in the pit he masti-cated incense leaves, spit on his hands, and rubbed them over his body. He entered the pit very early in the morning, and at once began to mutter wishes that eagles would come. Hawks, crows, and buzzards would come for the bait, but as soon as they alighted he would jab them with a sharpened stick. When an eagle came in sight, he knew it by the hurried departure of other birds. The eagle would wheel in great circles, high in the air, before descending, and never alighted directly on the bait, but paused at a short distance to observe if danger threatened. The hunter could hear the thump of its claws on the ground when it alighted. When the bird hopped upon the bait, the hunter waited while it tore at the meat, then very carefully and slowly put his hand through the hole, grasped both of its legs, pushed the branches

151

aside, and drew it downward. All this was managed very deliberately, and the bird scarcely struggled. The hunter grasped its neck, placed it across his knee, and broke the neck, while saying, 'I hope I shall catch a larger and better eagle than you!' Then with his foot he pushed the body into the end of the pit. Everything done in connection with catching eagles was deliberate and gentle. With good luck four or five were captured in a day. Seven were unusual, and ten about the maximum.

Toward evening the eagle-hunter crept out, laid the bait in the pit, and covered the opening from which he had emerged. Then he went home carrying his catch, walking very slowly, praying, and thanking his 'power' for success. Those who were already in his tipi remained, but no others could enter. At the back of the lodge in the place of honor he laid a bit of buffalo tongue and covered it with incense leaves of creeping cedar, and on this bed he deposited the birds in a row on their breasts with outstretched heads. In the beak of each one he placed a bit of pemmican (a mixture of pounded meat, fat, and dried berries). In front of them he made incense, and then covered them with a good piece of cloth or fur. . . . Then he took an eagle on his back, grasping its wings with his hands at his shoulders, and danced while four men whom he had engaged for this service sat in a row on the north side and shook [special] buffalo-hide rattles . . . and sang four songs. One of these ran: 'Good Eagle and all your children, give me wealth and health. If I get you and your children, I shall have many horses.' . . . The eagles lay in state during the night.

If no taboo were violated, the eagle-hunt continued at least four days, and if many birds were caught the kill of each day was laid on top of those previously taken. Should luck be good, the hunt was carried on six days.

Each time he returned after the first night, the hunter stood outside at the back of the tipi and prayed. When he was heard there, everybody in the tipi departed except his wife, who at once placed incense of sweetgrass on the coals in front of the eagles, first raising the sweetgrass to the four directions and then making four circular movements above the embers. The man then came around on the north side to the door, faced about to the east, and stood at the door. The woman knelt with bowed head on the south side. White clay mixed with crumbled sweetgrass was smeared on her hair. With a long stick painted yellow she pushed the flap aside and the man came in. At the same time she said, 'My children, I have the bed ready for you, and your food.' He passed around in front of her, lifting the eagles one by one from his back over the left shoulder. He made four circular movements with them in the incense, and then with four similar movements deposited them on the other birds. Any ruffled feathers he carefully and gently smoothed. The woman continued to sit in her place, reiterating, 'My children, I have a good bed and good food for you.' As before, the man put a bit of pemmican in each beak.

When an eagle-hunter had finished trapping, his wife cooked a large quantity of food the following morning, and all the people of every age were invited. The hunter sat in the place of honor in front of the incense fire; most of the other men were at his left and a few at his right. Mothers and children were mainly grouped near the door on the south side. The hunter sat quietly and prayed. The men at his left started an eagle song, and the others assisted while four men shook the rattles. In this way the first man sang four times, then those at his left in turn did likewise, while the same four men used the rattles. The songs were expressions of thanksgiving for success.

Then followed the feast, at the end of which the hunter, still sitting in his place, said, 'Now we will skin the eagles.' Each of the four rattle-shakers, in turn, stood up and recounted the brief history of the battle in which he had participated and in which an enemy had been killed without loss to the Sarsi. Then to the first of these four the hunter said, 'You will skin so many.' He divided the entire number of birds among these four men, who stepped forward one by one and took up the indicated number of birds, returned to their seats, spread blankets, laid the eagles on them, and removed from their beaks the bits of pemmican, which they put back in the place where the eagles had been lying. They proceeded then to skin the birds, being very deliberate, and careful that no feather became dislodged from the skin or disordered in any way. The claws were left attached to the skin. Then each of the four, and the hunter himself, piled the bodies on five pieces of red strouding, and the hunter placed with them some object pertaining to his wife and each of his children, such as an earring, a bead, or failing these a lock of hair. He then said to the first man of the four, 'I give you so many tail-feathers for helping me,' and handed him that number. Thus he paid each of the four. An entire skin he laid aside, saying, 'That is for the man who owns the rattles.' Then the five went out, carrying the pieces of cloth wrapped about the bodies. They went to a hill, and each one tied his bundle, along with bunches of white sage, to a stick lashed crosswise to the tip of a pole, which he planted in the ground. While thus engaged the four men prayed and the hunter himself cried as one who mourns for dead children. As soon as they returned, no matter how late in the night it might be, the people broke camp and moved away to rejoin the main band, all as if they had just disposed of the dead bodies of their children. The hunter removed all the feathers and claws from the skins and carefully wrapped them in bundles, and the skins he bound in a cloth and exposed on a pole set on a hill.

XVIII(1928), 95–98

Some Coastal Salish Fishing and Hunting Customs

Smelt and herring in open water are caught on the herring-rake, a thin wooden strip about eight feet long and three inches wide, with one edge for a space of about thirty inches set with a row of sharp bone teeth pointing slightly upward. The implement is whipped through the water as the fisherman's wife paddles through a school of small fish, and the creatures are impaled on its teeth, to be shaken off into the canoe.

A unique fishing lure consists of a wooden cylinder about two inches long with a socket at one end. About this end project three feather-shaped blades of white wood. The device is thrust far down into the water on the end of a long pole, and is then suddenly shaken off. As it rises, the blades impart a rotary motion, and the gleam of the white wood lures a cod from the bottom. As the fish comes into view, the fisherman hurls his spear.

Besides fish the most abundant sea foods are clams, mussels, oysters, crabs, sea-urchins, and sea-cucumbers. Of these the various species of clams are in greatest demand, and they are eaten raw, steam-cooked, or steam-cooked and dried in smoke and then eaten so or boiled. Cuttlefish is a delicacy highly prized, and roasted sea-urchins were considered the most palatable food a wealthy chief could serve at his feast.

The successful pursuit of porpoises and sea-otter required considerable skill. The former are yet hunted on moonlight nights as they sport in the smooth waters of some bay. The two hunters, spearsman in the bow and steersman in the stern, bring their little canoe silently toward the black, curving backs of the porpoises, tossing the drip of the paddles away in a thin, noiseless shower. The slightest noise of paddle on gunwale, of the harpoon taken in hand, of an inapt paddle-stroke, and the porpoises go down like a flash.

Whaling was practised by no Salish tribe of this region except the Quinault, and even among them there were only a few whalers. Evidently the art was derived from the Makah through the medium of the Quilliute, and the same methods were followed. The dead whale was towed ashore, the blubber was hacked off and rendered, the oil stored in hair-seal skins, and the flesh hung up in strips to dry.

Ducks, geese, and brant were usually captured in nets, which were used in several ways. A favorite method involved the use of firelight. On a clay-covered platform built above the stern of a small canoe a fire was kindled, and immediately in front of it stood the captain with his long steering paddle. Fastened to his shoulders was a light frame supporting a strip of matting, which extended from gunwale to gunwale and above the steersman's head, thus throwing the craft and its crew into deep shadow. On his knees the bow-man paddled silently and slowly, and the captain steered the canoe among the flocks of sleeping waterfowl. Attracted by the bright light the birds would swim toward it, but when they became aware of the canoe they whirled and swam away. Then it was, when the retreating birds collided with an on-coming flock, that the third man of the crew dropped his dip-net over the swirling mass of confused fowl.

Again, at the feeding grounds where herring spawned on sea-grass, a net about five feet wide and sixty to eighty feet long was suspended perpendicularly between poles set up outside the grass beds at low tide, being placed at such a height that at flood tide it would still be above water. As the tide rose the ducks would flock in to dive for herring spawn. Then a party hidden on shore suddenly rushed down to the beach, shouting and hurling missiles, and the affrighted birds squattered and flew straight out and into the net, in which their heads were held fast until the hunters came off in canoes and removed their catch. Nets of the same type were also stretched horizontally between two rows of stakes driven into the mud flats above a bed of green hemlock boughs, the butts of which were thrust obliquely into the mud. At flood tide the boughs and the net were submerged. The herring spawned on the hemlock, and ducks, diving outside the net, would swim under and feed on the roe, and then rise straight upward, to run afoul of the meshes of the net and drown before they could extricate themselves.

At narrow, timber-lined waterways, such as the mouth of a stream at the sea or at a lake, or as a narrow channel connecting

64 *Homeward*, one of Curtis' early prizewinning photographs taken on Puget Sound near Seattle

two inlets, nets of very fine nettle or hempen fibre or sinew cords were stretched high in the air between two trees or two tall poles, to entangle the fowl as they flew along their accustomed highway to or from their feeding grounds.

Gulls were killed in great numbers by the children, principally for their down, which was used in the manufacture of blankets. Teeming flocks of these birds would congregate at the mouths of rivers to pick up refuse from the up-stream camps, and during the salmon run they would follow the school to feed on dead fish. Into such flocks the Indian boys would hurl stones with their slings, frequently killing or wounding several birds with a single missile. Excessively cruel, even among primitive practices, was one of their methods of killing gulls. A double-pointed wooden skewer was thrust down the gullet of a herring, which was then cast into the water for the gulls. The stick, lodging in a bird's crop, resulted in strangulation or in a more lingering death by starvation. Among the Twana it was a favorite pastime of the children to prepare herring in this fashion, sharpening hundreds of little cedar sticks for the purpose. The women of the tribe in need of gull-down had only to paddle along shore at any time to find all the birds for which they had any use. The Clallam children, and their cousins across the straits on Vancouver island, snared many gulls. Little wicker squares were made from split willows, and upright sticks at the four corners held the loop of the snare spread. In the centre was tied a herring, and the device was then sunken and anchored with a stone, so as to be a little below the surface of the water. A gull flying above would catch sight of the bait, dive for it, and come up with its neck in the noose, which quickly tightened and choked the bird. IX(1913), 51,54–57

The Klamath Staple Diet

The staple article of food was the seed of the yellow water-lily, *Nymphæa polysepala*. It is still used as a delicacy. The extensive marshes of the region are in many places covered solidly to the extent of hundreds and thousands of acres with the spreading leaves of this plant. *Wokas*, as the plant and the seed are called, is gathered in the latter part of August and through the whole of September. Poling a canoe through the masses of leaves and trailing stems, the harvester, always a woman, pulls the nearly ripe pods from their stems and drops them in the canoe. The mature pods, having burst open, are too sticky to be taken in the hand, and are scooped up in a tule ladle and deposited in a canoe-shaped basket. At the end of the day the contents of the basket are poured into a pit about two feet in diameter and of equal depth, and from day to day the harvest of ripe pods is added. The whole is covered with a mat. At the end of the season the contents of the pits, now by fermentation a viscous mass, is transferred to a canoe, and after the admixture of water it is thoroughly stirred

so as to separate the seeds, which drop to the bottom. The gluey liquid and refuse are skimmed off, and the seeds are drained on mats. After more thoroughly drying and partially cooking the seeds by shaking them in a tray with a few embers, the woman cracks the hulls with muller and metate, and separates the kernels from the hulls in a winnowing tray, which is operated with much the same motions as a gold-miners' pan. The finished product is now ready to be thoroughly dried on mats and stored, formerly in pits, now in bags. The seeds are prepared for eating by parching them with embers in a basketry tray (the frying-pan is used at present), a process which causes them to swell and burst. It may be eaten so, a food of excellent flavor, or covered with cold water. The immature *wokas* pods, which constitute by far the greater part of the daily harvest, are spread on the ground to a depth of six to eight inches, and in about ten days those exposed to the sun are dry enough to be crushed on a mat with a stone pestle, after which the seeds are winnowed in a tray and stored. The pods that have not been exposed to the sun have partly decomposed, and the sticky mass is crushed where it lies and spread more thinly to facilitate drying. Later the seeds are winnowed in the usual manner. The seeds derived from immature pods are prepared for eating by parching, removing the hulls on the metate, and boiling into a mush in a cooking basket by means of heated stones. This method of cooking has of course been superseded by more modern processes. In order to avoid waiting for the sun to dry them, the pods gathered near the end of the season are roasted in a fire, crushed into a gluey mass, and dried by admixing pulverized decayed wood or ashes, after which the seeds are separated by screening and winnowing.

XIII(1924), 167–168

10 War and The Chase

The Tiwa of Taos: War Customs

Three or four days were spent in preparing weapons and moccasins for a hostile expedition. Arrow-points were dipped in menstrual or puerperal blood, which also was placed under the sinew wrapping. Such blood was dried and kept for this purpose. At the first camp they gathered in a circle about the fire and prayed and sang to Bear, Cougar, Weasel, Moon, asking for strength, courage, cunning, favorable weather, good luck. Returning, they sent one or two ahead with the news, telling how many scalps and how many child captives had been taken.

The young men then set out to meet the warriors, and when they were seen approaching, the war-party set up the scalp-pole and the young men, mounted, rushed up to it, shooting at the scalps and striking it with sticks. Together the two parties returned to the village, where all the older men gathered outside the walls and received a detailed report of the battle and what each warrior had accomplished. That night the warriors and the other men of the village assembled to make and practise new songs referring to the fight.

The next day the warriors painted their bodies and faces black, loosened their hair, and scattered eagle-down on the head. . . . An equal number of [them] painted the body and face red, loosened the hair, and put eagle-down on the head. The scalps hung at the top of a pole, around which these two parties danced, yelling, shooting, gesticulating, reviling the enemy, menacing the captives huddled about the base of the pole. From various houses came old women, screaming and menacingly shaking their fists. Arriving at the circle, they rushed in and mistreated the captives, pulling their hair, kicking them, spitting on them, reviling their tribesmen. Then all the other women came and participated, all ululating. The women danced outside the circle of warriors, stepping quickly up and down without progressing, and holding the hands at the shoulders with elbows at the sides. Their faces were blackened. The men danced in the fashion characteristic of Plains Indians, making threatening gestures, sometimes firing their guns, holding up their shields on the left arm. Other than the painted dancers with the warriors,

men did not participate; but if a man were seen at a distance watching the dance, two or three warriors or their companion dancers captured him and led him to the plaza, where he was compelled to dance until his women ransomed him by bringing a basket of food. This dance continued four days, starting rather early in the morning and lasting until after dark, with intervals of rest and feasting. The warriors spent the night together in any kiva, where they ate only meal in its various forms. Long before dawn they marched through the streets, singing, and after breakfast resumed the dance. On the fifth morning, very early, they secreted the scalps among the rocks outside the pueblo.

Relations with alien tribes were by no means of a uniformly hostile character. Annually traders in considerable numbers camped near Taos to exchange buffalo-skins for the products of the country. Though they were compelled to leave the walled village before dark, their relations with the Taos females were of such a friendly nature that today the average Taos physiognomy and figure are those of Plains Indians, a similarity heightened by the white cotton sheet worn by all Taos men and boys. An informant declares that he was one of a party which, returning from a visit to the southern Cheyenne about 1897, introduced this Cheyenne garb at Taos. It was so favorably received, largely because an individual so enshrouded could prowl about in his nocturnal philandering without recognition, that it quickly became a tribal badge; and now pressure is brought to bear on returned schoolboys who are slow to adopt it. XVI(1926), 38–41

Professional Warriors of the Coastal Salish

It was principally for the purpose of taking slaves and plunder that war was prosecuted. Seldom did pitched battles occur, and these usually were fought in canoes. Generally their fighting consisted in lying in ambush for a small, unsuspecting party, or in carrying the women and children away from a village while the male population was absent. As trophies of individual prowess, heads of the slain were invariably brought home and impaled on short poles in front of the village until they had become bleached skulls, when they were thrown aside. In decapitating an enemy, a man always was careful to call the attention of some comrade, in order to have a witness when he should boast of his deed.

67 *Waiting for the Signal—
Nez Percé*

Certain men of fierce, determined mien were known as professional warriors to whom all things other than murder and pillage were mere avocations. Their faces were covered with black, even in times of peace, and their eagle glance caused other men's eyes to seek the ground. A man of this class it was who organized a war-party, in which any man, whether or not a professional fighter, might enlist.

The weapons of a warrior were bow and arrows, yew spear with point of bone, and a simitar-shaped club of stone or whalebone about fourteen inches long and somewhat sharpened on the convex edge. [They wore a] protective wooden corselet. . . . The quiver of wolf-skin with the hairy side exposed was worn at the hip. One form of head-dress consisted of a number of eagle-feathers so arranged as to stand upright in a straight line along the top of the head; another was a mass of feathers covering the head, with a pair of eagle-feathers upright at the back; and among the Cowichan there is found a peculiar variety consisting of the entire scalp and hair of an enemy.

After equipping themselves and blacking their faces with charcoal, the members of an expedition stood shoulder to shoulder on the beach and sang to embolden their hearts, while dancing up and down. Cowichan warriors, in several ranks and with weapons in hand, would advance slowly while chanting in unison, repeating the words of their leader.

At the conclusion of the dance and the song of encouragement, the men leaped about, imitating the act of paddling, and then embarked and paddled away without a backward glance. A short distance from home they landed, to lie in concealment until evening; for war-parties usually travelled only in the dark.   IX(1913), 75–76

Bear Impersonation among California Indians

The Yuki shaman first dreamed of bears, and then was instructed by them. The Pomo bear-men possessed the strength, cunning, and swiftness of bears merely by wearing bear-skin suits; and they killed, principally among their own people, for mere pleasure. Among the Kato these personators of bears are said to have confined their depredations to hostile tribes, and like the Pomo they claimed no relations with the bear spirits. How much truth there is in these statements can no longer be proved. However, considering the frequency of the known use of bear-skin costumes by tribes outside this area, it is entirely possible that these bear personators actually existed, and only their fabulous instruction and exploits are imagined.

Certain active men, say the Kato, were trained to personate bears, and those who proved the swiftest runners were provided with bear-skins cut to fit the body and stitched together. The skin was stiffened with a lining of slats of yew, so that arrows could not pierce it. The tongue was a piece of abalone-shell on a deer-skin thong; for a grizzly-bear's lolling tongue is said to be noticeably shiny. Sometimes two long pieces of obsidian or flint were stuck into the eye-sockets, for the avowed purpose of piercing an enemy if the bear-man happened to dash into him. The bear-shamans carried long knives, and sharply crooked yew staffs with which to catch the ankles of enemies fleeing in the brush. Sometimes, but not always, several of these men would accompany a war-party. They would send scouts to an enemy village, to listen outside the houses at night and learn where the people were going on the following day; and at that place they would lie in wait. Or if they found a place where deer-snares had been set, they would conceal themselves there.

In the summer succeeding the training of new bear-men, a war-party including the bears and two young women would invade the enemy's country and remain there for a long time. When they started out, or perhaps before that, a certain old man would rub bear's dung vigorously across the abdomen of these

163

women, and they would quickly conceive and produce cubs. It is quite possible that a pair of cubs was actually captured and passed off as the progeny of the women. When it proved very difficult to find the enemy in a situation favorable for attack, they would tie these young bears in the undergrowth, and the enemy, hearing them cry, and coming to capture them, would fall an easy prey to the marauders. It is said that these bear-men could approach quite closely without detection. They were greatly feared, and men always tried to elude rather than to resist them, perhaps because it was impossible to pierce their armor. They were called *nonihlsai* ('bear dry,' perhaps in allusion to the drying of the rawhide suit), and like bears they ate roots of the plant *nonich-paghecho*, which was supposed to make them overwhelmingly strong.

XIV(1924), 8–9

Apsaroke: The Death of Iron Eyes (as related by Hunts to Die)

Bull Rises Small and Blackbird On The Ground raised a war party against the Lakota to avenge the death of ten Apsaroke, who had been killed some time before. Iron Bull was in this party. He was always doing strange things, yet he afterward became chief. Probably it was he who had the warriors of the party ride through the camp before dusk, their women behind them, stopping before different groups of lodges, singing the song that was always used before leaving for war against the Lakota. The swiftest runners among them were wearing long wolf-skins whose tails swept the ground. I went out for my horse and began to saddle. My father usually said nothing when I wished to do anything, but now he said, 'My son, from the time I was born to this day never have I known our warriors to sing the war-songs in broad daylight. Something will happen to these people. Do not go.' So I threw off the saddle.

Iron Eyes sat in the midst of his friends, and his father, No Neck, came and beat him on the breast, and cried, 'My son, when your friends have fear on their faces and weep within themselves, and run this way and that before the enemy, stay behind and fight! Do not come back! Death comes, and you cannot leap over him. I want to cry before I am old!'

There were many great fighters in that party, and one of the greatest was Big Otter. He was the chief who would call the young men to him and try their bows, and if they were not good, break them, and say, 'Go to a certain man and have him make you a good bow. Pay him.' He would test their other weapons in the same way. With the seventy warriors were five women and a child, and three boys learning how to fight.

Passing near the country of the Hidatsa, they turned southward and on the fortieth day camped at the foot of Rainy Hills, [South Dakota]. Scouts informed the chiefs that in the east they had seen the smoke of four fires. Everybody began to paint, but Bull Rises Small said, 'We know that many sit around one fire. There are four. This day we will be no more!' They left their women and boys at the foot of the hills, and went on to the east toward the camps of the Lakota, some of whom were already on their way to the west, a great hunting party, and the two passed each other without knowing it.

The enemy came upon the women, children, and horses. Two of the women, the little child, and the three boys escaped; the other three women and the entire camp outfit were captured. The last band to leave the villages was attacked by the Apsaroke, who got there just about that time. Our men killed two or three, scalped them, and withdrew, when another large party came and struck them. In the first fight the Apsaroke had become divided into three parties, two of which made their escape from the field. In the third party were forty or forty-five men. They rode rapidly toward where they had left their women and children, but they were set upon continually by fresh parties of Lakota returning from the attack on the women and boys.

As they retreated, fighting, Iron Eyes and Bull Rises Small, who were mounted on fine horses, would turn and hold the enemy for a moment, then dash forward and join their friends, who in the meantime had got a good start. At last Bull Rises Small leaped from his horse, and, dodging from side to side, shot at the charging enemy. The Lakota surrounded him, dashing around and back and forth, and finally killed him. They covered him up with their numbers and came on. Then Iron Eyes would turn and hold back the enemy alone. His friend, Three Thighs, was put on the ground by a shot through his horse's hip, and Iron Eyes took him on his own horse. Then he shouted, 'My friends, I have helped you long enough! My flesh is hot with running, and I go no farther! The words of my father No Neck are sticking in my throat! Tell him for me that I died like a brave man!' When the Lakota came close enough to hear, he sang the Apsaroke death-song, the one a man uses when he is going to dismount and hold the enemy.

Just then Only Boy found himself afoot, and called on Iron Eyes for help. He also was taken on the horse, and then Iron Eyes leaped down and shouted to the others to go home and tell his father how he died. The others wheeled the horse and jumped off, slapped it in the face, and stayed with him. Three more men turned their horses and went back, leaped down, and stayed: Iron Eyes was not the only brave man. These three were Big Forked Horn, Loin, and Golden Eagle. They were surrounded by Lakota, a great swarm, while the most of them continued the chase. It took a long time to kill those six. Iron Eyes was left lying alone nearest to the Lakota camps.

Big Otter was in another division of this large party, for they

had become further separated in the retreat. As the enemy pursued them, he looked back and saw a man pointing, and directing his warriors. He said, 'I will see if he is a man, that person who talks and points!' and leaping from his horse, he went back. The Apsaroke stopped, and the Lakota held back as their chief jumped down and came forward to meet Big Otter. He put an arrow to his bow and shot as he ran. Big Otter ducked his head and the arrow struck on the top and glanced off high into the air. The Lakota shot again, striking him in the shoulder. Big Otter fired his gun, a flint-lock, but the powder had fallen out, and the bullet merely rolled out of the barrel. He threw the gun behind him and ran forward, and before the Lakota could draw another arrow from his quiver, Big Otter grasped him by the left wrist. The Lakota raised his bow and began crying aloud. He was afraid to die. Big Otter was a strong, big man. He pulled out a long knife, and taking his enemy by the throat, plunged it into his breast and ripped him open through bones and flesh down the breast and out to the side below the ribs. Then he gave him a push and the man fell, and all his entrails gushed out on the ground. Big Otter turned away and walked toward his friends, then looked back, and shouted, *Lakota biukate, navadhi!*—'Come on, Lakota women!' But when they gathered around their chief and saw what that strong man had done, they signed to him, 'Go on!' and cried for the dead man. Big Otter mounted behind a friend who had ridden back, and they went on.

The whole prairie was dotted with little parties of Apsaroke retreating before swarms of Lakota. In another band of our men was Strong Falcon. His mother's brother jumped from his horse and cried out, 'Strong Falcon, when you get home to the

Apsaroke camp, whose horses are you going to ride?' Strong Falcon had taken care of his horses and ridden them, and he meant that he was not going to return home, but would die there. The young man at once turned back and dismounted beside him. They were quickly surrounded, and the older man was soon killed. Strong Falcon kept on fighting, and as his medicine began to manifest itself—it was bear—his teeth came out between his lips and froth was on his mouth. He rushed at the Lakota, just like a mad bear; they fell back, and finally ran and left him.

In that day's fight eighteen Apsaroke were killed or captured, including the women and children. Many Lakota were killed.

When the warriors got back home they sneaked in at night like whipped dogs. No Neck came to the lodge of the first one, and asked, 'How is it?'

'Many will not return,' was the answer.

'Tell me about Iron Eyes,' said the old man; 'how did he act?'

'The last time I saw Iron Eyes he was facing the Lakota, fighting to give his people a little time to run; then I saw a hundred Lakota surround him and from a hill I saw him covered by the enemy.'

No Neck tried to laugh, and started to walk to his lodge, but stumbled and fell. When he was alive again he took a knife and slashed his arms and legs. 'Iron Eyes, Iron Eyes, I did not know it would be this heavy or I would not have said what I said! I thought it was a good thing when I said, "Stay behind!" but, my son, it is bad!' So he wept and cried. The wife of Iron Eyes wore a dress covered to the ankles with elk-teeth, and two long strings of them hung from each ear. As soon as she heard the mourning of No Neck, without waiting to take off her elk-tooth dress she seized a knife and stabbed her head many times, and slashed her arms, so that the blood ran over her clothes. Every night after that No Neck sat in his lodge, weeping, and crying over and over, 'Iron Eyes, and the bay horse with the split ears, I shall never see you again! I did not know it would be this way. If I had a hundred sons, none would be like you, Iron Eyes, Iron Eyes, my son!' All night he would wail such words, and the whole camp heard them, and the hearts of the young men became hot against the enemy. In the day-time he was alone in the hills, mourning. His hair was shaved close, and he wore nothing but a piece of old lodge-covering. As he sat with his head on his knees, the magpies would perch on his shoulders and peck at the old buffalo-skin, and mountain-rats gnawed holes through it. For more than two years he mourned thus, until a great victory was won over the Lakota. Then for the first time he washed the blood from his face.

IV(1909), 97–101

II Mythology

A Wiyot Myth of the Origin of the World

... '[A]bove old-man' was alone. There was nothing but water. He thought there should be people and some land for them to live on. So he made the land, but it was barren. He thought it did not look right, because it had no trees and no grass. So he made vegetation on the earth. Then he made people. These people were not good; they quarrelled and talked ill, so he sent a tidal wave and drowned all except two, Shatash (condor) and his sister. These two, knowing that a flood was coming, had made a large storage basket, and in it they floated about on the water. When the water subsided, the man went to look for food, and to observe the country. When he came back he said, 'My sister, are you home?'

'Yes,' she answered. But she would not say, 'Yes, my brother.' Seeing that she would not address him, he became suspicious that she might not regard him as her brother. One day he returned from his travels and said to her, 'Are you here, my wife?' Then she laughed. She liked it.

So this man married his sister, and they were the ancestors of all who afterward peopled the earth.

XIII(1924), 190–191

Eskimo: The First Woman comes to King Island

A woman, the first person to come to King Island since it had been made from a fish, came ashore. No one knows whence she came, nor how she got there. The woman built a hut of grass and cut up much meat for winter food. After being there some time she noticed that the carcasses, as she cut them, came to life and bled from their noses. Then morning after morning, on waking, she found part of her parka-hood gone. She knew some one had been with her, but could never discover anybody. At last, waking suddenly, she saw a man beside her. She said: 'You have been coming here all fall and winter. I did not see you or know who you were.'

'I felt sorry for you,' answered the man, 'because you were alone, so I stayed with you. You and I are married. Now I must hurry; it is light, and I may be too late to see some one.'

The man always brought her much meat. The woman knew that her husband was Polar Bear.

Then many seal were left for her, which she cut up and stored away. She knew that some one else was hunting for her, but neither she nor her husband could learn whom. One night Black Whale in human form entered, very angry because Polar Bear had married the woman. His gifts of seal had been his suit. The two fought in the house. Polar Bear Man cried: 'There is not room to fight here; let us go outside!'

They struggled on the beach in their own forms, Polar Bear snapping with teeth and slashing with claws. Whale lashed out viciously with his tail. Polar Bear lodged himself on Whale's back and sunk his teeth in Whale's nose. With furious energy Whale vainly tried to dislodge Bear. Exhausted finally, and crying, 'I can fight no longer, I am giving up!' Whale dived in the sea.

Polar Bear once more became human and lived peacefully with his wife.

XX(1930), 105

Jicarilla: The Origin of Fire

Black Man, Haschin Dilhili, was created by Nayenayezgani to be his helper in the task of making the earth a good dwelling-place for the people. Haschin made the animals, mountains, trees, and rivers, gave the people weapons and implements, and showed how they were to be used. When all were supplied with houses to live in and weapons with which to protect themselves

70 *A Primitive Quinault* wearing the costume traditional for women of most Coastal Salish peoples

and to kill game, he called Coyote, Tsiliten the Mimic.

'Go to the Land of the Fireflies,' he commanded, 'and bring back their fire, for the people have no fire with which to cook their food.'

Coyote started, and found the Land of the Fireflies. These beings lived at the bottom of a deep, deep hole—an enormous cave in the solid rock. Its sides were smooth and straight, and how to get down Coyote did not know. He went to the edge of the pit, and there found growing Little Tree.

'Help me down to the Land of the Fireflies,' he said. So Little Tree sent its roots down, down, down, until they extended quite to the bottom, and Coyote descended. There he played with the little Firefly boys, romping about, running back and forth, pretending to be thinking of nothing but their amusement, for the Fire-flies guarded their fire carefully and would let no one touch it.

On the tip of his tail Coyote had tied a tuft of cedar bark. Suddenly he dashed through the great fire which always burned in the centre of the village, and was off before the Firefly people knew what he had done. When they discovered that he had stolen some of their fire, they set out in pursuit; but Coyote was very swift of foot, and reached the wall of the pit far ahead of them.

'Little Tree, help me out!' he called.

Little Tree drew its roots up, up, up, while Coyote held on and was drawn safely out of the hole. Then he ran quickly about among the people, lighting the piles of wood they had prepared, until every family was supplied with fire.

I(1907), 69

Shasta: Horsefly Outwits Thunder

Thunder and Horsefly lived together. Every night Horsefly brought home much blood, and Thunder one night asked, 'Where do you get all that blood?' Horsefly reflected for a moment, and said, 'Oh, I suck it out of trees and out of the ground.' Then Thunder thought, 'I will try that way to get food.' He struck a tree, but found no blood. He tried another. He tried every kind of tree, and then the ground in many places; but there was no blood. He said to Horsefly, 'I do not believe you get blood from trees and the ground.' But Horsefly only repeated that it was so; for he feared to tell that he sucked blood from people, lest Thunder, in trying to get blood, strike them dead.

XIII(1924), 206

A Kutenai Deluge Myth

One day Chicken-hawk's wife, Pheasant, went to pick berries. About mid-day, tired and hot, she went down to the lake for a bath. No sooner was she in the water than she saw Ya-woo-nik, a water-monster, and she was frightened. As she hurriedly swam to the shore, he called to her not to be frightened, for he was not going to harm her. Then she stopped, and he made love to her. She gave him all her berries, and remained with him until it was

late. Afraid to go home without berries, she went to the mountains and hurriedly gathered some fruit, breaking off leaves and twigs in her haste. When she reached home, her husband asked at once why she had brought such berries, and she replied that she had had a headache and had not been able to gather clean fruit.

Chicken-hawk was suspicious, and on the next day he followed her. While she picked berries, she sang happily, and gathered clean fruit. About noon she had a great quanity and went to the lake, still gayly singing, and at the shore she threw the berries into the water. Chicken-hawk, keeping close in order to see what she was doing, beheld the monster coming through the water. Ya-woo-nik ate the berries, and Pheasant stood on the shore singing. Then she went into the water.

Chicken-hawk hastened home, to mend his arrows and to look after his bow. In the evening his wife returned again with trashy berries, and with her head bandaged, feigning headache. Chicken-hawk made no complaint.

On the next day he followed her again; saw her quickly gather berries and carry them to the lake; saw the monster eat them and then came ashore to caress her. At that moment Chicken-hawk put an arrow through his body. Water began to stream forth from the wound, and it spread and rose higher and higher. All creatures fled to the mountains, and Chicken-hawk put one of his tail-feathers into the ground to mark the rise of the water. When it reached the last stripe, it stopped and receded. Had it passed that mark, it would have destroyed them all.

Hopi: The Corn-Smut Maid

People were living in the village which now is in ruins on the knoll north of Tawa-pa. There was a youth named . . . Rainbow youth who daily practised running before sunrise and made offeringa of pahos in order to become swift and strong. Otherwise, day and night, he remained in the house. He was handsome.

One day he let it become known that he would never marry, unless it should be a girl whose meal was so fine that it would adhere to the . . . abalone-shell that hung in his house on the wall. Then all the maids in the surrounding villages began to grind meal, making it as fine as possible. For all the girls wished to marry this handsome youth.

A girl of Awatobi was the first to come for the trial. Rainbow Youth was kind and courteous to her. He invited her into the house, and after a time he asked, 'What is it you wish?'

'I have come for you,' she answered.

'*Anchaai*!' said the youth. He opened the cloth that contained the girl's meal and threw some of it against the shell, but it did not adhere. 'I cannot go with you,' he said, 'because your meal will not adhere to my [shell]."

'*Anchaai*!' answered the girl quietly, and departed.

In this manner many others failed.

There was a girl at Kuchaptuvela named Nana-mana ('corn-smut girl'), who was swarthy and dirty. Her brothers told her that they did not think Rainbow Youth would consent to come with her, even if her meal should stick to the shell; nevertheless, she said that she would try. She took some of her meal and went to the young man's house. He invited her to enter and sit down, and he asked what she wished.

'I have come for you,' she said.

'*Anchaai*!' he responded. He took some of the meal and threw it against the shell, and it stuck fast. He said again: '*Anchaai*! It is my word. I have agreed to go with the girl whose meal stuck to my [shell], and your meal has done so. Therefore I go with you.' So they went to the house of Nana-mana.

Her brothers and mother were surprised, but no less pleased. Toward evening Nana-mana went into an adjoining room, but she did not reappear. Another person came out, a beautiful young woman, and Rainbow Youth wondered who she was. About bedtime the brothers began to speak to her, and gave him to understand that this was really their sister and his bride, Nana-mana. Her former appearance had been due to a mask that she wore during the day; every day she wore the mask, but at night removed it and revealed her true self.

Now the other girls who had been rejected were angry and made sport of Rainbow Youth and his dirty bride. But the young man was not annoyed, for he knew that his wife was really beautiful. After he had lived with her for some time, she said that since she was a supernatural being she would leave the people. So with all her family she disappeared into the ground, and the place where she disappeared is now the shrine of Nana-mana.

72 *Kotsuis and Hohhuq.* These mythical birds, whose vast beaks are controlled by wires, are servants to a man-eating monster during the Kwakiutl winter ceremonial sequence

Teton Sioux: Myth of the White Buffalo Woman

Many generations ago, when Lakota still dwelt beside the lake far away in the east, they experienced a winter of terrible severity. The snow lay deep on the ground, and the streams were frozen to their very beds. Every day could be heard the sharp crack of trees as the frost gnawed at their hearts; and at night the piles of skins and the blazing fires in the tipis scarcely sufficed to keep the blood coursing through the veins. Game seemed to have deserted the country, for though the hunters often faced the hardships of the winter chase, they returned empty-handed, and the wail of hungry women and children joined with the moan of the forest. When finally a tardy spring arrived, it was decided to leave a country so exposed to the anger of Waziya, Spirit of the North, and seek a better homeland in the direction of the sunset, where ruled the Wing Flappers, who existed from the beginning.

There was little enough to pack besides tipis and fur robes, and what few dogs had not been eaten were soon harnessed to the laden travaux. Two young men were sent in advance. No pair could have been more different in their nature than these two, for while one was brave, chivalrous, unselfish, and kind, the other's heart was bad, and he thought only of the sensuous and vicious.

Unencumbered as they were, the scouts were soon far ahead of the wearily dragging line of haggard men, women bent under burdens that dogs should have been drawing, straggling children, and a few gaunt dogs tugging at the overladen travaux. Late in the day the scouts succeeded in shooting a deer, and thinking their people would reach that point for the night's camp, they left it where it had fallen and were turning away to seek other game when one of them felt a sudden impulse to look back. Wonderful sight! There in a mist that rose above a little hill appeared the outline of a woman. As they gazed in astonishment, the cloud slowly lifted, and the young men saw that she was a maiden fair and beautiful. Her only dress was a short skirt, wristlets, and anklets, all of sage. In the crook of her left arm she carried a bundle wrapped closely in a red buffalo-skin; on her back was a quiver, and in her left hand she held a bunch of herbs. Straightway the young man whose heart was evil was overpowered by a desire to possess the beautiful woman, but his companion endeavored to dissuade him with the caution that she might be *waka* [sacred] and a messenger from the Great Mystery.

'No, no!' he cried vehemently, 'she is not holy, but a woman, human like ourselves, and I will have her!'

Without warning he ran toward the woman, who forthwith warned him that she was a sacred being. When he persisted and went closer, she commanded him sternly to stop, for his heart was evil and he was unworthy to come near to the holy things she bore. As he still advanced, she retreated, laid her burden on the ground, and then came toward him. Suddenly it appeared to the waiting youth that the mist descended and enveloped the mysterious woman and his companion. Then followed a fearful sound of rattling and hissing as of thousands of angered rattle-snakes. The terrified observer was about to flee from the dreadful place when the cloud lifted as suddenly as it had descended, disclosing the bleached bones of his former comrade, and the beautiful virgin standing calmly beside them. She spoke to him gently, bidding him have no fear, for he was chosen to be priest of his nation.

'I have many things to impart to your people,' she said. 'Go now to the place where they are encamped, and bid them prepare for my coming. Build a great circle of green boughs, leaving an opening at the east. In the centre erect a council tipi, and over the ground inside spread sage thickly. In the morning I shall come.'

Filled with awe, the young man hastened back and delivered to his people the message of the holy woman. Under his direction her commands were reverently obeyed, for were they not a message from the Great Mystery? In the morning, gathered within the circle of green boughs, they waited in great expectancy, looking for the messenger of the Mystery to enter through the opening left at the east. Suddenly, obeying a common impulse, they turned and looked in the opposite direction, and behold! she stood before them.

Entering the tipi with a number of just and upright men selected by the youth whom she had chosen to receive the sacred rites, she at once spread open the red buffalo-skin, exposing its contents—tobacco, the feather of a spotted eagle, the skin of a red-headed woodpecker, a roll of buffalo-hair, a few braids of sweet-grass, and chief of all, a red stone pipe with the carved image of a buffalo calf surmounting its wooden stem. At the

73 *A Smoky Day at the Sugar Bowl* in Hoopa Valley, a place 'so beautiful that it is mildly astonishing that [the Hupa] Indians have been allowed to remain in possession'

same time she explained that the Great Mystery had sent her to reveal to them his laws, and teach them how to worship, that they might become a great and powerful people.

During the four days she remained with them in the tipi she instructed them in the customs they were to observe—how the man who would have great *waka* power should go into the high places and fast for many days, when he would see visions and obtain strength from the Mysteries; how to punish him of evil heart who sinned against the rights of his brother; how to instruct girls at maturity, and to care for the sick. She taught them also how to worship the Great Mystery by selecting, in the summer of each year, a virgin who should go into the forest and cut down a straight tree; this was to be dragged in and erected for the Sun Dance, but before the ceremony all the virgins should come up and touch the pole, thus proclaiming their purity. But

175

a false declaration would be challenged by the young man who was able to testify to the transgression and she should be driven from the place in derision. A young man wishing success in war or love should paint a rock and make a vow that in the coming dance he would offer himself to the Mystery: then whenever he saw this rock he would be reminded of his vow.

Then she taught them carefully the five great ceremonies they were to observe: . . . the Foster-parent Chant, the Sun Dance, the Vision Cry, the Buffalo Chant, and the Ghost Keeper. The sacred pipe she gave into the keeping of the chosen young man, with the admonition that its wrapping should be removed only in cases of direst tribal necessity. From the quiver on her back she took six bows and six arrows, and distributed them among as many young men, renowned for their bravery, hospitality, and truthfulness. These weapons she bade them take, after her departure, to the summit of a certain hill, where they would find a herd of six hundred buffalo, all of which they were to kill. In the midst of the herd would be found six men. These also they were to kill, then cut off their ears and attach them to the stem of the sacred pipe. Her last words were these:

' So long as you believe in this pipe and worship the Mystery as I have taught you, so long will you prosper; you will have food in plenty; you will increase and be powerful as a nation. But when you, as a people, cease to reverence the pipe, then will you cease to be a nation.'

III(1908), 56–60 With these words she left the tipi and went to the opening at the eastern side of the camp-circle. Suddenly she disappeared, and the people, crowding forward to see what had become of her, beheld only a white buffalo cow trotting over the prairie.

The Legend of the Navaho Happiness Chant

The Happiness Chant is a nine-days' chant held inside a hogan, and like many of the Navaho ceremonies, it was derived from another tribe. The myth relating to it tells of a renowned warrior who had two beautiful sisters whom he wished to see married, but only to men who should first prove their strength and valor in a feat of arms; so word was sent to all the young men of the warrior's tribe to gather at his home on a certain day, prepared for war, if they wished to enter a contest he would then propose. The girls being coveted prizes, a goodly number of warriors, painted and dressed in full war regalia, assembled on the appointed day, among them being two old, white-haired brothers, of an alien tribe, who had recently come to live near the Navaho people. The young chief protested at the presence of the old men, declaring that they would only sacrifice their lives in the first combat, for they could have no possible hope of success. The two persisted, however, and were allowed to remain in the van.

Four-days journey from the Navaho country was a village of the . . . Have Holes For Houses, enemies from early times. They also prided themselves on having two very beautiful girls, upon whom many admiring young men of the tribe bestowed valuable presents of turquoise, shell beads, and other jewels. One of these wondrous beauties wore her hair plaited always with rich strings of turquoise; the other with strings of white shell.

'To the two men,' said the vaunting young Navaho, 'who will fight their way to the homes of these boasted beauties and bring to me their jewel-plaited scalps, will I give my sisters.'

The band started, each man eager and hopeful, and on the fourth night bivouacked in sight of the cliffs under which the hated [enemies] had their homes. At daybreak on the following morning they made their attack on the pueblo, but the villagers, ever alert and well prepared for an onslaught, offered desperate resistance, every man fighting bravely for his life and his family. All day long the contest raged; arrow, lance, and stone hammer dealing death on every hand. As nightfall shrouded the combatants in darkness, the invaders, depleted in rank, slunk back to their camp on the hill, where they found the two gray-haired brothers, each bearing a jewelled scalp as his trophy.

When the Navaho chief learned that the old men were the victors, he raged with anger, condemning his tribesmen and vowing that his sisters should never become the wives of unknown aliens, and accordingly declared a new contest. The man who would win a beautiful wife must hit the blade of a yucca plant with an arrow at forty paces. The long, narrow blade was hung in the bark of a tree and the contest commenced. The younger men shot first. One by one they twanged their bows, and one by one marched off in sullen humor. At last it came the turn of the aged brothers. The first shot his arrow, and the slender leaf was pierced, the second shot, and again the leaf was pierced, but so soon as the second arrow had hit its mark the Navaho declared a new feat, contending that this had not been sufficient. A long race was then arranged, and once more the brothers came off victorious.

The chief became desperate. Some feat must be devised in which his own men could prove superior. In the wall of a high cliff not far distant was a small hole, barely larger than a half-closed hand, and just above the reach of the average man. The ones who could run past the hole, jump, and thrust their hands into it as they did so, might claim the sisters. One by one the young Navaho warriors leaped wildly and struck out for the hole in the cliff, but none could thrust his hand into it. Then the elderly brothers ran past, sprang lightly, and darted a hand each into the pocket.

But for the third time the Navaho chief declared the test insufficient. The cliff was high. They who would marry his sisters

must shoot an arrow over its rim; so a second contest in archery took place, but only the feathered reeds of the white-haired brothers passed out of sight.

Still the old men were refused the prizes they had fairly won so many times. A dance was called. Finding no way to outdo the two brothers in skill or strength, the young chief left the selection of husbands to his sisters. They should join the men in the dance and go home with whom they chose. The aliens did not join the dancers, preferring instead to remain in their own little brush house half a mile distant, with its single-slant roof, 'For it is foolish,' said one, 'to think that two such handsome young maidens as they are would ever look with favor upon our rags and wrinkles. We would better lie here to-night and rest in sleep after our busy day.' Each then brought forth a sacred pipe and tobacco, which they used only on rare occasions. One had a pipe of rich blue turquoise, and the other one of fine, pure white shell. They filled them, smoking in silence. From the distance the songs and laughter of the merry dancers greeted their ears, but not as joyous sounds. Each smoked with apparent resolution, blowing forth cloud after cloud of filmy whiteness, and lo! as they smoked each noticed that the other had grown youthful in appearance! Their tattered garments, too, as insensibly as the creeping shadows, changed their forms, becoming fine shirts, leggings, and moccasins.

At the dance the younger sister asked, 'What is it that smells so sweet?'

'I have noticed nothing,' the other replied.

'Come over here and face the breeze,' said the first; and there, sure enough, came wafts of air sweet and savory. Neither

had ever before scented anything so pleasing, and they determined to follow the aroma against the breeze. The moon shed
ample light to guide their footsteps, and once locating the true
direction whence the wind came, the two had no difficulty in
threading their way straight to the home of the brothers who
had vanquished so many rivals in so many feats. Knowing
nothing of the men, other than that they were strangers from
an alien tribe, the girls were somewhat startled at coming so
boldly face to face with them; but a moment's hesitation gave
them assurance, for surely, they thought, such finely dressed,
handsome men could mean no harm.

Said one: 'What it was we did not know, so came to determine
if we could; but the most delicious odor we ever smelled
seemed to fill the air about us at the dance, coming always from
this direction, and now we see that it was the smoke of your
tobacco. It must be a wonderful land, where you come from, if
tobacco like that grows there.'

'That you may see for yourselves,' answered the elder brother,
for we have come to take you there if you will but consent to go.
Our land is rich in jewels and possesses a soil that grows bountiful
crops of many kinds, some of which you have never seen.
Marry us and you shall live always in abundance.'

The girls consented, and at bedtime retired with their husbands
for the night, only to waken in the morning, however, to a sense
of horror; for whom should they find beside them but the two
grim-visaged old men so cordially hated by all their tribe! They
dared not to display their fear and horror before the men, who
were quite awake, though feigning sleep, but each read the
other's feelings at a glance. Where were they? Where had they
been? Had they merely dreamed of meeting two handsome,
well-clad strangers in the night? Slowly their memories came
back—the last shooting contest, the preparation for the dance,
the songs and feasting, the enchanting perfumed breezes, and
their quest—they remembered now. But how this change in
their companions? They were strangers, and unquestionably
magicians who could transform themselves or work spells on
others! With this thought the desire for vengeance increased
with every pulse-beat.

The day wore on before the women had a chance to talk
together apart from their husbands, when they agreed that they
would return to their home and tell their brother of the evil
worked upon them by the old men, whom they would then soon
see killed; but the Little Whirlwind whispered to them, 'Return
not to your home; anger fills the hearts of all your people, and
it is you who would be killed with clubs and stones.' Thwarted
in this plan, they determined to leave and search for a distant
tribe of which they had once heard, that lived in peace, and had
never led the life of marauders. There, surely, they might receive

food and shelter and freedom from the sorcery of their husbands. Each would take a separate course upon starting, to meet at a wooded mountain in the east.

All went well throughout the day; the old men rested and made ready for the journey to their home-land, on which they planned to start at daybreak. That night the women did not sleep. When their husbands became wrapt in slumber, they quietly crawled out from their furs, snatched a little food, and glided into the moonlight. They had been gone but a short time when one of the old men arose to stir the fire, and in deep surprise noted the absence of the women. He called his brother, and the two held a hurried consultation. They circled the lodge, but in the dimness of the light could discern no guiding foot-print to tell the direction in which their young wives had gone. Returning to the camp, they filled their sacred pipes, and in silence sat and smoked. Soon a thin curl of smoke was seen drifting southward, winding in and out among the piñons; then another on the north side. These they followed, bearing eastward, smoking as they went, and as the sun began to tint the purple shadows, they came upon their wives in a little rocky cañon screened by thickly growing cedar and piñon. The smoke foretold the women of their doom, so they were not taken by surprise.

Seeing no way to escape, the girls resigned themselves to fate,

and meekly followed the old men back to camp, whence they journeyed with them to the west.

At their home the brothers had wives and children, so they did not herald their new consorts as such, but wedded them at once to their eldest sons. This prospect pleased the two young women, and they entered into the spirit of the new life with zest. They learned the songs and chants of the rites of the Snake and the Bear people—the clans to which these younger husbands belonged—and taught them to a young brother who came to visit them. When the brother returned to the Navaho people, he told them that his sisters were quite happy, and with the songs he had learned from them he originated the ... Happiness Chant.

I(1907), 106–111

Coastal Salish: The Jealous Husband

A certain man who was jealous of his pretty young wife went with her one day to bathe, but instead of going into the river near the village, he took her up the stream to a lake. She did not know where this lake was, and after walking a long time she became uneasy and asked, 'Have we not gone far enough?' But he forced her to go on, and when at last they reached the lake he said, 'Climb that hemlock and break off some branches with which to rub our bodies.' She climbed up, looked down, and asked, 'Am I high enough?' 'No, go higher!' he commanded. Again she paused and again he sent her higher. 'Go to the top,' he called, 'for the top has more power!' When she was in the very top, where the tree

75 The Sun Dance Encampment—Piegan

bent with her weight, he said, 'That is high enough.' Then he himself climbed up after her and bound her in the crotch of the tree. As he descended, he cut off all the branches close to the trunk and stripped off the bark, and there he left her in the tree while he went home.

The woman had four brothers, who were shooting ducks on the bay. Though they were so far away, she could hear them, and she began to sing, 'Come, brothers, I am growing weak with the heat!' The youngest brother said to his brothers: 'Stop . . . listen to what I hear! I think it is our leader.' They went ashore and walked rapidly toward the sound. When the reached the foot of the tree and saw their sister, the eldest twisted a rope of cedar withes and made a tree-climbing apparatus. He started to climb, but slipped and fell. The woman was now dead with the fierce heat of the sun. The second brother and the third tried, but both fell. Then the youngest took the rope and climbed to the top. He called down, 'What shall we do? She is dead!' 'Throw her down,' they said. He did so, and they removed her bracelets and anklets, and put them on the eldest brother. Then he put on the skirt, trying to act like the woman; but he was not successful. Each in turn tried it, but though each did it better than his predecessor, only the youngest was perfect. This was a part of their plan to kill their brother-in-law. They buried the body there. . . .

After completing their plans they went home. The youngest, dressed in his sister's garments and ornaments, sat down outside the house, and, as he had seen his sister do, he took off the skirt and loused it. A little boy, seeing him, went in and said to his mother, 'The wife of my chief is outside.' 'Call her in,' she said. So the child called the youth. It was dusk. They gave him fern-roots, which he placed in the fire and roasted, just as he had seen his sister do. He took them out and beat them with a stick to loosen the skin. A boy sat watching him and said, 'Why, she has a man's hands!' But the woman, who was the sister of the dead woman's husband, nudged the boy to keep silent, for she knew there had been a quarrel between the couple. Yet again the boy said: 'Look at her! She has a man's hands!'

After the youth had finished eating, he went to bed with his brother-in-law, and they lay back to back. After a while the man turned and put his arm around his supposed wife, but the youth groaned and pushed his hand away, saying: 'My body is sick. You had better go to sleep.' So the man slept. Then the youth drew his knife from its concealment under the skirt, turned quietly over, and slashed the man's throat. He cut the neck all around, twisted off the head, covered the body with mats, and went out carrying the head by its hair. He went home and set it in the place of honor.

In the early morning the four brothers fixed the head on the end of a pole, which they thrust through the roof at the front of the house, so that everybody could see the gory thing.

When the dead man did not appear that morning his parents looked into the bedroom, and seeing blood dripping from the bed they sent the dead man's little nephew to call his uncle and tell him that his wife was having her menses. The boy went in, seized the mat, and jerked it off, crying, 'Do not stay here!' Then he saw the headless body and ran out shouting, 'There is no head on that body!' He began to sing:

'Ai yai! Did I not tell you that she had a man's hands?'

12 Songs and Tales

A Teton Sioux Love Song

Look, my husband I do not love;
Tell him (my lover) I will live with him.   III(1908), 150

Kotzebue Eskimo: The Trader

A woman was so occupied with her new-born child that she could not
accompany her husband to the nightly winter dances in the men's house,
although she sometimes stood by her own door to listen to the singing
as it was wafted by the wind. One night, while sitting alone with her
child, she was surprised to see a strange man appear suddenly through
the doorway. His clothes were rich, but his face was black from exposure,
hunger, and thirst, and his body was thin. He signed for water, and drank
a bucketful without stopping. He gulped a huge quantity of meat. Now
that his throat was clear, speech flowed easily. The stranger presented
the woman with a large bead set on a string of beads in return for the
hospitality. He said that he had been storm-blown from Siberia and had
landed at this village, but he was so ashamed of his appearance that he
kept hidden, living in a grave-box. The woman repaired his boots,
which were in tatters from ice cuts, and gave him small pokes of meat,
oil, and water. She offered to make two more pairs of boots which
would last until he could return home.

She said nothing to her husband of the stranger. That one returned the
second night for more provisions, and for the first pair of boots, which
were finished. His body had filled out somewhat, and his face seemed
less pinched and blackened. He watched her sewing, and then went back
to his place of concealment without saying a word.

On the third night the village held a feast and dance for a recent
arrival, which the husband attended, while his wife remained at home.
She stood by her doorway for a while, listening to the singing from the
men's house, then went inside to finish the second pair of boots. The
Siberian soon entered, and said, as he took the new boots: 'I give you
thanks for your aid. I am well and strong once more. Next summer you
and your husband must make your camp on that point of land across
from this village. I shall be with the Siberian boats which will visit
there. I shall bring gifts for you and your husband.'

As he left, the woman gave him much meat, berries, oil, and water.
When her husband returned after the dance, she showed him the beads
and told of the Siberian. He was vexed, and exclaimed: 'Why did you
not let me know? I should have given him all new clothes!'

'His clothes were very good, all but the boots. I fed him until he was

77 A Kotzebue Eskimo wearing
clothes of modern material
which have been tailored
in the traditional manner

well, and sent him away with plenty of provisions,' rejoined the wife.

The husband grumbled: 'You should have told me. I should have
given him many furs.'

During the winter and spring, the husband obtained more sealskins
and oil than he could use. When the ice was out, he re-covered his skin
boat, and with his family and household belongings sailed for the point
of land designated by the Siberian. There they fished all summer.

One day, when a fine on-shore wind was blowing, he made out sails
approaching his camp. The Siberians, amongst whom the woman
recognized the man she had aided, soon made a landing and were
welcomed and feasted. Then the boats, containing much wolverene,
furs of all kinds, tobacco, pots, and knives, were unloaded. That night
the Siberian retold the story of the woman's kindness, and added: 'I have
brought wolverene and spotted deer fur as a gift to her, and tobacco for
her husband for that aid. In thanks for the new boots, I shall offer some
pots and knives. But for that help I should not be alive, and my parents,

who were very glad that I returned, have also sent gifts.'

Man and wife stowed away that which they had received; they and the Siberians traded for a long time. The Siberian gave the husband trade goods to use in the village, saying that he would return the following summer.

When the couple arrived at their village and attended the dances and games, they traded these goods for furs. At that time a knife was worth three white fox; a large pot, six fox-furs; and a roll of tobacco, one fox. This couple made fine clothes for themselves. In the following summer they returned to their camp, and later again met the Siberian with whom they traded furs for goods. The two men became partners and traded every year in this manner.

XX(1930), 191–192

Comanche: The Woman who betrayed her Husband

In a camp there lived a woman with her husband and four brothers· One night a hostile tribe raided the camp and stole the woman. The husband and brothers took up the trail with the intention of rescuing her, following until they reached the hostile camp. Once there, the husband posted the brothers in a cottonwood grove, while he hid himself near the water-hole, for he knew that his wife would come there sooner or later.

78 *Dusty Dress—Kalispel*

After many had come and gone, and when his patience was nearly at an end, the wife came to the hole for water. When he had signalled her to where he lay in hiding, she appeared glad to see him. After they had finished their talk, she said that she would take the water to her captor and then return to go home with him.

The wife went up to her captor, whom she had married in the meanwhile, and told him of a dream that she had had. She said that she dreamed of four enemies hidden in a grove of cottonwoods near the creek, and of another hidden near the water-hole. She said that this man was her former husband, and she described how he was dressed. She begged that if her dream was true, they would not hurt the husband. The captor and some warriors surrounded the grove and killed the four brothers, while they captured the husband. That night they treated him roughly, playing many tricks on him, while his wife urged them on in their language. Then they set up two poles and hung him from them by his wrists. In the morning the camp broke up, leaving the husband to die suspended from the poles.

When all were leaving, one old woman hung back, apparently looking around the camp for anything of value that might have been left behind. She came to where the man was hanging, and said: 'I have a son who looks just like you. For his sake, I shall cut you loose.'

She cut him down and gave him a horse to enable him to get back home.

XIX(1930), 193

Oto: Why it does not pay to Steal

At one time the people used to turn their horses loose, all together in a drove, so that when spring came there would be many colts, which would belong to the owners of the mares which the colts followed. One man, believing himself to be sharper than the rest, figured ahead so closely that he was with the herd when the young ones were born. He observed that his colt, a bay standing by its mother, had a drooping ear, for which reason he thought it was not any good. He picked out a spotted colt, perfect in every way, and changed the two about, neither colts nor mothers noticing the difference. Then when the villagers turned out to get their ponies, he took the spotted colt and brought it home. Everyone admired it and said he was lucky to get such a foal. He felt quite proud of what he had done.

But during the first year the bay's ear grew straight and he became a fine-looking horse in every way. After training and gentling, he defeated all other horses in the races, even the spotted one, though he was fast too. Later the bay beat all the horses of other tribes and won a great reputation.

The tricky man did not feel so elated now, so he began to plan how to recover his bay horse. He thought to himself, 'That is my horse, and I must find a way to get it back.' He thought that way all day and all night and all the time.

At last he took the spotted horse and two others to the lodge of the bay's owner and said: 'That bay horse you have is really mine. I stole him and substituted the spotted colt. Now you have had him long enough, and to pay for keeping and training him I shall return your spotted horse and give you two others.'

The good man merely laughed and laughed, while others, seeing all the horses before one lodge, began to gather around. The good man looked about and said: 'A while ago this man stole a horse from me—the spotted one. Now that he sees what a good one he lost in swapping unknown to me, he brings back my horse and two others for the animal that was his in the first place. So I shall give him back his horse and get XIX(1930), 168 my own and two others besides. Sometimes it seems good to steal, but stealing never turns out well in the end.'

Kalispel: Turtle Races with Frog and Eagle

A large number of animal-people were in camp together, competing in foot-races. Frog and Eagle had proved the best. Near by in another camp lived the Turtle brothers, sixteen of them, and they all were as like as so many berries. As the eldest looked on his fifteen brothers and noticed that they were exactly alike, he had a thought. 'Let us go to the races to-morrow, and run against Frog,' he proposed. Then he unfolded his plan, and the others agreed that it was good.

They arrived about nightfall on the following day. The camp was on the shore of a small, clear lake, along the edge of which grew tall grass. In the darkness the eldest Turtle arranged his brothers at equal intervals around the shore of the lake, and bade them lie close in the grass.

At daybreak, when the people began to assemble at the race-course, they saw Turtle laboriously crawling about and heard him calling a challenge to race. Knowing him to be the slowest of all creatures, they thought he was only joking, and asked him if he wished to run against the champion Frog. 'Yes, it is true,' he answered, 'I wish to race with Frog.' In great glee they called to Frog: 'Here is the swift Turtle, who wishes to run with you! Are you not afraid of him?' 'We will run at noon,' answered

Frog. When the time came, there were not many wagers laid, for all were afraid to bet on Turtle; but a few backed him, regarding the whole affair as a great joke. Said Turtle to Frog, 'I will bet against your tail: if you lose, I will take it and wear it.' Frog agreed.

The two stood ready, and at the word they started. Frog soon took the lead, but he did not hurry, for he felt confident he would win. Looking back, he could not see his opponent, but in front he heard a voice calling him, and there was Turtle ahead of him, creeping industriously around the lake. Again he passed Turtle, but again, on looking behind, he could not see him, and again the creeper appeared ahead of him. Time after time this happened, and Frog, being slow of wit, did not know he was being cheated. As he neared the end of the course, there a little in front of him was Turtle crossing the line. The winner dropped on a pile of the wagered blankets and pretended to wipe the perspiration from his body; then he took his knife and cut off Frog's tail. Frog, ashamed of his loss, sat quiet, unable to move about without exhibiting his shame, and at last he leaped into the water, saying that he would forever remain where his disgrace might be concealed.

Then said Turtle: 'I will beat two good racers to-day. I will beat Eagle!' 'Will you race with me!' asked Eagle, incredulously 'Yes, I am willing to race with you, and I shall beat you,' said the other. Then the others began to think that Turtle must be a runner after all, and they staked wagers on him. When all the bets had been made, Eagle said, 'Where shall we start, at the beginning, or half-way around!' 'Half-way around', answered Turtle, 'and in the air.' 'But how are you going to get up into the air!' asked the other. 'You shall carry me into the air,' said Turtle. To this Eagle agreed, thinking, 'I wonder how Turtle will get down without killing himself. We will start from not very high, so that he will not be hurt.'

So Eagle carried Turtle up to about the height of a tall tree; but his opponent insisted that it was not high enough, so up he went still farther. When they had gone quite high, Turtle said, 'Put my head down, and when I am ready, then let me go, and we will both race to the ground.' Eagle was still anxious lest Turtle be killed, but when the word came, he released his hold and down shot Turtle. And after him swooped Eagle, trying to catch him, for he thought surely he would be killed in striking the ground. But he could not grasp the slippery body. Turtle struck on a heap of buffalo-chips, but Eagle was afraid to strike the ground, and glided away without alighting. As Turtle arose and began to wipe his eyes, he saw Eagle still in the air, and at once claimed the race, for he had reached the ground first. Eagle protested that he had not been fairly defeated, but the others decided in favor of Turtle. VII(1911), 111–112

Chinookan: Coyote's Slaves

A war broke out on the river, and Coyote participated, capturing two slaves, both small persons. 'I am going to have something different from the others,' thought he. He took them home and set one down on each side of his house. The next morning he saw that one of his slaves was beginning to swell, and he notified the people in the village that something was wrong with him. The swelling continued, until the slave seemed ready to burst, and about midnight he did burst, the explosion wrecking the house. Not knowing what had happened, Coyote began looking for his slave, and he decided to call on his medicine for advice. His medicine was his feces, which he called his 'two sisters.' They were very wise, knowing always what was occurring. They told him that the slave he had had in the house was West Wind, and Coyote could not find him again because he had gone back to the place in which he had been found. But when snow fell, Coyote was to trap him, setting a snare wherever he saw a black spot on the hillside. When winter came, Coyote saw a small black spot on the snowy hill, and there he set a trap. On the next day he saw the same small person caught in the trap by the hand, and he brought the captive back to his house; but again the slave blew up, destroying the house. This time his medicine told him it was of no use to try to keep this person a slave. 'He is very important,' it said. 'He lives up in the hills, and whenever he

79 *Oasis in the Bad Lands—* Teton Sioux

comes, the snow goes away. If you had killed him, the winter would never end.' So Coyote had only one slave, and that was Flea. After the fight in which he was captured, Flea was in the bottom of the canoe in which the fighters were returning home, and he was so small that another slave sat down on him without seeing him, which made Flea flat.

VIII(1911), 123–124

Sitting Bull's War Song

This song was used by Sitting Bull when the warriors, mounted, sat awaiting the word to charge. Riding back and forth along the line, he would repeat the song in a high, shrill voice:

> Earth all over they name me;
> I am doing all I can, you must do your best.

III(1908), 149

A Teton Sioux Brave Heart Song

> Heart-hard (my) friend long ago has gone;
> I survive him.

III(1908), 148

Bibliographical Notes

Works by Edward S. Curtis

Curtis' principal work was *The North American Indian*, 20 volumes of text, including many photographs, accompanied by 20 portfolios of large photographs (Cambridge and Norwood, Mass., 1907–1930). Volume One contains a Foreword by Theodore Roosevelt, the texts were edited by Frederick Webb Hodge, and patronage was provided by J. Pierpont Morgan. Curtis also wrote two popular books titled *Indian Days of the Long Ago* (New York, 1914) and *In the Land of the Head Hunters* (New York, 1915), a series of articles for *Scribner's Magazine* (1906–1909), and other essays, mostly on Indian themes. A number of his photographs appear in the reports of the Harriman expedition to Alaska edited by C. Hart Merriam, *Harriman Alaska Series*, 14 volumes (New York and Washington, 1901–1910), as they do in such journalistic pieces as his own 'The Rush to the Klondike over the Mountain Passes', *Century* (March, 1898), 692–697.

Works on Curtis

The most important early comments on Curtis appear in an essay written by his friend and mentor George Bird Grinnell: 'Portraits of Indian Types', *Scribner's Magazine*, XXXVII (March, 1905), 258–273. With the exception of an article-interview by Edward Marshall— 'The Vanishing Red Man', *The Hampton Magazine*, XXVIII (May, 1912), 245–253, 308—most of the other early articles were superseded by several essays written by Ralph W. Andrews in the early 1960s, and especially by his *Curtis' Western Indians* (Seattle and New York, 1962), which includes extracts from *The North American Indian,* correspondence, and photographs. Andrews' work has been augmented somewhat by T. C. McLuhan's Introduction to a selection of Curtis' photographs, *Portraits from North American Indian Life* (New York, 1972; London, 1973), by Douglas C. Ewing's article on the inception of *The North American Indian,* ' "The North American Indian" in Forty Volumes', *Art in America* (July–August, 1972), 84–88, and by Don D. Fowler's commentary to *In a Sacred Manner We Live: Photographs of the North American Indian by Edward S. Curtis* (Barre, Mass., 1972). A further selection of Curtis' pictures appeared in an Aperture book *The North American Indians* (New York, 1972; London, 1975). Brief interesting comments on *In the Land of the Head Hunters* (1914), Curtis' film, appeared in W. Stephen Bush, 'In the Land of the Head Hunters', *The Moving Picture World,* XXII (19 December, 1914), 1685, and in Vachel Lindsay, *The Art of the Moving Picture,* rev. ed. (New York, 1922; reissued, 1970), p. 114.

Works Quoted in this Selection

Chief Seattle's comments in the Introduction are taken from the version printed in T. C. McLuhan's anthology (which includes Curtis photographs), *Touch the Earth: A Self-Portrait of Indian Existence* (New York, 1971; London, 1973). In the text itself David G. Burnet's and Robert S. Neighbors' comments on the Comanche were taken from H. R. Schoolcraft's *Indian Tribes of the United States,* 2 volumes (Philadelphia, 1860), G. P. Winship's description of Alvarado's reception at Acoma from his *The Coronado Expedition* (Washington, 1896), and John Muir's memoir of an encounter with the Mono from *The Mountains of California* (New York, 1894). Other quotations were taken directly from Indian informants, with the exception of comments by a Secretary of the Interior on the human and financial cost of the Indian wars; these came from the *Report of the Commissioner of Indian Affairs,* 1868 (Washington, 1868).

80 An *Ogalala War Party* re-enacts, for Curtis' camera, days gone by

Index

In parentheses after each people referred to its linguistic group followed by its geographical location is given as witnessed by Curtis. Cross-references and page numbers of illustrations are italicised. Roman type indicates a mention of the people; bold type indicates pages where the people is treated in detail.

Koskimo A *Kwakiutl* tribe, *85, 178*
Kotzebue A division of the *Eskimo, Alaskan,* 183-5, 77
Kutenai (Kitunahan; Idaho, Montana-Canadian border country) 114-16, 136-8, 170-2, *137*
Kwakiutl (Wakashan; coast of British Columbia) **32-6,** **84-8, 142-4, 149-51,** *12, 35, 69, 85, 110, 143, 173, 178*

Laguna (Keres; Rio Grande Valley, New Mexico) *46*
Lakota See *Teton Sioux*
Leκwiltok A *Kwakiutl* tribe, 32
Luiseno (Shoshonean; San Luis Rey River drainage, southwest California) 114

Makah A *Nootka* tribe, 155
Mandan (Siouan; N Dakota) 16, 56
Mishongnovi A *Hopi* pueblo, 45
Miwok (Penutian; hills and coast of western California above the Fresno River) 109-11, 37
Mohave (Yuman; Colorado River, northwestern Arizona, Fort Mohave, Arizona, Needles, California) 113, *95*
Mono (Shoshonean; Mono Lake to Owens Lake, California) 36-9, 190, *38*

Nakoaktok A *Kwakiutl* tribe, *173*
Navaho (Athapascan; northeast Arizona, southwest Colorado, northwest New Mexico) **122-8, 129-33,** **176-81,** *12, 43, 88, 12, 105, 126, 130*
Nez Percé (Shahaptian; Idaho, Washington) 68-71, 9, 16, *161*
Nisqualli A *Coastal Salish* tribe, 66, 106
Noatak A division of the *Eskimo, Alaskan, 102*
Nootka (Wakashan; west coast of Vancouver Island, British Columbia and Cape Flattery, Washington, the latter known as *Makah*) 101-2, 108, *32, 33*
Ninivak A division of the *Eskimo, Alaskan,* 20, 139, 141, 142, *19, 115, 138*

Ogalala A division of the *Teton Sioux,* 52, 81-2, *82, 184*
Oraibi A *Hopi* pueblo, 45, 46, 88, 90
Osage (Siouan; western Missouri, Kansas, Oklahoma) *72*
Oto (Siouan; Missouri, thence to Indian Territory, Oklahoma) 185-6, *83*

Pakavi A *Hopi* pueblo, 45, 90
Paiute Term used of the various peoples of Shoshonean linguistic stock living in the Great Basin. 23
Papago (Piman; southern Arizona and Sonora, Mexico) 16, 50, *67*
Paviotso (Shoshonean; western and northwestern Nevada and northeastern California) 39, 59, *150*
Pawnee (Caddoan; Platte Valley, Nebraska, thence to Indian Territory, Oklahoma) 18
Pecos (Tanoan; Rio Grande Valley, New Mexico) 22
Piegan (sometimes loosely referred to as *Blackfeet* or *Blackfoot*) (Algonquian; Montana and Alberta) 55-8, 146-7, 11, *56, 64, 180*
Pomo (Hokan; coast and hills of California to the north of San Francisco Bay) 163
Ponca (Siouan; Nebraska, thence to Indian Territory, Oklahoma) 76
Pueblo Term used to designate the town-dwelling *Keres, Tewa, Tiwa* and other communities (usually excluding the *Hopi* of Arizona) of the southwest, such as *Acoma, Hano, Jemez, Pecos, San Ildefonso, Taos,* and *Zuñi.* 22, 24 -5, 74, 130

Quilliute (Chimakuan; Olympic Peninsula, Washington) 155
Quinault A *Coastal Salish* tribe, 155, *169*

Salish See *Coastal Salish* and *Interior Salish*
San Ildefonso (Tanoan; Rio Grande Valley, New Mexico) *62*
Santo Domingo (Keres; Rio Grande Valley, New Mexico) 65-6
Sarsi (Athapascan; Alberta) 133-5, 151-4
Shasta (Hokan; northern California and southern Oregon) 170
Shipaulovi A *Hopi* pueblo, 45
Shongopavi A *Hopi* pueblo, 45
Shoshoni (Shoshonean; northern California, Nevada, Utah, Wyoming) 21, 52-3
Sia (Keres; Rio Grande Valley, New Mexico) *160*
Sichomovi A *Hopi* pueblo, 45
Sioux See *Teton Sioux (or Lakota)*
Songish A *Coastal Salish* tribe, 100-1
Spokan An *Interior Salish* tribe, 148
Suquamish A *Coastal Salish* tribe, 67

Taos (Tanoan; northern New Mexico) 159-61, 74, *45*
Teton Sioux (or *Lakota*) (Siouan; ranged out from the Dakotas and Wyoming) **79-84, 173-6, 183,** **189,** 9, 40, 52, 53, 113, 146, 164-7, *17, 119, 123, 184, 188, 190*
Tewa The division of the Tanoan linguistic group which includes such peoples as those of *Hano* and *San Ildefonso,* 43, 46
Tiwa The division of the Tanoan linguistic group which includes such peoples as those of *Taos*
Tsimshian (Tsimshian; coastal region of northern British Columbia) 32
Twana A *Coastal Salish* tribe, 157

Ute (Shoshonean; ranged out from Utah) 43

Walapai (Yuman; Grand Cañon, Arizona) 43, *13*
Walpi A *Hopi* pueblo, 45, 47, 107, *44*
Washo (Hokan; Lake Tahoe region, California and Nevada) 58-9, *58*
Wichita (Caddoan; Oklahoma) 61-5, 94-6, 23, 73, *97*
Wiyot (Algonquian; Humboldt Bay, California) 168

Yakima (Shahaptian; Washington) 16
Yokuts (Penutian; San Joaquin Valley, central California) 135-6, *136*
Yuki (Yukian; Round Valley, western California) 163
Yurok (Algonquian; Klamath River Valley, northern California) *60*

Zuñi (Zuñian; western New Mexico) 91-4, 43, 47, *93*